WHY SAILORS CAN'T SWIM

And other marvellous maritime curiosities

WHY SAILORS CAN'T SWIM

And other marvellous maritime curiosities

NIC COMPTON

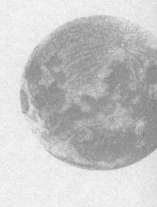

ADLARD COLES NAUTICAL

BLOOMSBURY

LONDON · NEW DELHI · NEW YORK · SYDNEY

Published by Adlard Coles Nautical
an imprint of Bloomsbury Publishing Plc
50 Bedford Square, London WC1B 3DP
www.adlardcoles.com

First edition published 2013

Print ISBN 978-1-4081-8805-7
ePub ISBN 978-1-4081-9263-4
ePDF ISBN 978-1-4081-9264-1

A CIP catalogue record for this book is available from the British Library.

This book is produced using paper that is made from wood grown in
managed, sustainable forests. It is natural, renewable and recyclable.
The logging and manufacturing processes conform to the environmental
regulations of the country of origin.

Created and produced by Ivy Contract
SENIOR EDITOR: Judith Chamberlain-Webber
ART DIRECTOR: Kevin Knight
DESIGN: JC Lanaway
ILLUSTRATION: Ivan Hissey, John Woodcock

Typeset in Generis Serif Com and Univers

Printed and bound in Great Britain by CPI Group (UK) Ltd, Croydon CR0 4YY

NOTE: while all reasonable care has been taken
in the publication of this book and to ensure
accuracy, the publisher takes no responsibility
for the use of the methods or products
described in the book or for any factual errors.

Contents

Foreword

What do people remember about Nelson? The fact that he thrashed the French at the Battle of the Nile, slaughtered the Danes at the Battle of Copenhagen and chased the French and Spanish fleets across the Atlantic? Or that he died at the Battle of Trafalgar and may (or may not) have asked his second-in-command to kiss him before he breathed his last?

And what about yacht racing? Do people know or care about the latest legal wranglings over the America's Cup? Or the fact that Conny van Rietschoten is the only sailor to have won the Volvo Ocean Race twice? Or are they more interested in the 'upside-down sailor' Tony Bullimore, who got stuck in his overturned boat in the middle of the Southern Ocean, and a fresh-faced Ellen MacArthur (right), openly weeping after having to climb the mast yet again on the last leg of her legendary round-the-world voyage?

The truth is, we like stories about people. We like anecdotes and quirky tales – which is what this book is full of. You won't find any long-winded histories of yachting races or detailed analysis of wetted surface area and angles of heel. Just some great yarns, good old-fashioned drama on the high seas and plenty of stories that don't often get told.

I hope you enjoy reading it as much as I enjoyed writing it!

Sailors & superstitions

THE ULTIMATE RACE

IT WAS BILLED AS THE RACE OF THE CENTURY: a contest to see who would be the first person to sail around the world single-handed and non-stop. Several sailors were already preparing for the voyage when the *The Sunday Times* announced its Golden Globe challenge: a trophy for the first person to complete the circumnavigation, and a £5,000 prize for the fastest. The only stipulation was they had to start and finish from a British port between 1 June and 31 October 1968. In the end, there were nine starters (six British, two French and one Italian), of whom four retired before leaving the Atlantic. Of the rest, Chay Blyth retired after rounding the Cape of Good Hope, Donald Crowhurst committed suicide while faking his journey, Nigel Tetley's boat sank while in the lead and Bernard Moitessier opted out. There was only one finisher: British Merchant Navy officer Robin Knox-Johnston (later Sir), who completed the loop in 313 days. Nearly 40 years later, Sir Robin was at it again. Aged 68, he came fourth in the 2006–07 Velux 5 Oceans race, finishing in 159 days. He didn't mind not winning this time because, as he said, 'You can't break my record.'

The sea has never been friendly to man. At most it has been the accomplice of human restlessness.

Joseph Conrad, Polish/British author (1857–1924)

WHY DO SAILORS WEAR EARRINGS?

Traditionally, sailors who had rounded Cape Horn wore a gold loop in their left ear – the ear closest to the Cape on a typical eastbound voyage – as a sign of their achievement. Sailors are also said to have worn earrings to pay for their funerals should they fall overboard and their bodies be swept ashore. In ancient times, gold earrings were supposedly worn to pay the ferryman to carry you across the River Styx to the afterlife. Gold earrings were also thought to have healing powers and to improve eyesight – which sounds a bit mad until you find out there's an acupuncture point in the ear that relates to vision. Another likely reason sailors wore earrings is that timeless obsession: fashion. Sailors just thought they looked good.

CONSIGNED TO THE DEEP

It was, and still is, commonplace for sailors who died on a voyage to be buried at sea. If there were casualties during a battle or if a ship was sailing in some far-off place, it made no sense to transport bodies – with all the associated health risks – back home for burial. Adding weight to this view was an old superstition that claimed that carrying a dead body on a ship slowed it down. Typically, a body was stitched up in canvas, weighed down with a suitable ballast such as cannonballs, and after a short service, consigned to the deep. According to tradition, the last stitch of the shroud was usually passed through the nose of the corpse, to ensure the person wasn't just sleeping.

MODERN SEA BURIALS

BURIALS AT SEA are becoming popular once again, and the US Navy receives about 500 requests per year for them from former personnel. According to the US Environmental Protection Agency, bodies must be buried at least 3 miles (5km) away from land and in at least 600ft (180m) of water. If using a casket, it should be weighted with 4lbs (1.8kg) of extra weight for every pound (0.5kg) of body weight and drilled with six 3in (8cm) holes to prevent air getting trapped. In the UK, caskets must be made of softwood such as pine and must not contain any plastic, copper, zinc or lead. British authorities require 40–50 holes to be drilled in the casket. Alternatively, you can purchase an Atlantic Sea Burial Shroud from New England Burials at Sea, priced at $1,750 USD plus shipping.

Famous people buried at sea

Mariner and explorer, Sir Francis Drake, in a lead coffin off Panama, 1596; US newspaper magnate, EW Scripps, from own yacht off coast of Liberia, 1926; drummer with the Beach Boys, Dennis Wilson, off California, 1984; actor, John Carradine, off California, 1988; Al Qaeda leader, Osama bin Laden, from USS *Carl Vinson* in Arabian Sea, 2011 (disputed by some). Of the 328 bodies recovered after the sinking of the *Titanic*, 119 were too badly damaged to be identified and were buried at sea.

Famous people whose ashes were buried at sea

HG Wells, Steve McQueen, Janis Joplin, Rock Hudson, Gene Kelly, John F Kennedy Jnr.

HOLD FAST

TATTOOS ARE THOUGHT to have originated among the indigenous tribes of the Pacific and were brought to the West by early explorers. Captain Cook and his crew were probably the first Westerners to experience them and coined the word tattoo from the Polynesian *tattow*. They were extremely popular among 18th-century sailors and certain images acquired special symbolism. For example:

ANCHOR – for crossing the Atlantic (also used for serving in the Merchant Navy).

FULL-RIGGED SHIP – for rounding Cape Horn.

TURTLE/KING NEPTUNE – for crossing the Equator.

DRAGON – for serving in Asia.

PALM TREES – for serving in the Mediterranean (Royal Navy) or Hawaii (US Navy).

HULA GIRL – for serving in Hawaii (US Navy).

HARPOON – for working on a fishing boat.

SPARROW – for every 5,000 miles (8,000km) at sea, to help you find your way home.

STAR OR COMPASS ROSE – to help find your way home.

HOLD FAST – one word across the knuckles of each hand; to prevent falling overboard and/or prevent you letting go of a line.

PIG AND ROOSTER – to prevent drowning; supposedly, pigs and chickens were kept in wooden crates that floated when a ship sank, which meant that they stood a better chance of survival.

SAILOR JERRY LIVES ON

You may not know who Sailor Jerry is, but the likelihood is that you've seen one of his tattoos or something closely based on them. Sailor Jerry, real name Norman Collins, was a legendary tattoo artist based in Hawaii and is widely recognised as the father of modern tattooing. Collins was a US West Coast drifter who picked up his tattoo skills in Chicago in the late 1920s and practised his art on fellow-drifters. He joined the US Navy aged 19 and eventually fetched up in Hawaii, where he set up what would become a tattoo haven in the seedy heart of Honolulu. He fused bold American designs with a more subdued Asian palette to produce distinctive designs that were soon copied the world over. He was also an innovator and perfectionist, who developed his own range of safe pigments and insisted on high standards of hygiene. After his death in 1973, his business was developed into the Sailor Jerry range of clothing and gifts featuring Collins's tattoo work – including a range of Converse trainers. The business later added rum to its range and, labelled with a tattoo-style hula girl, Sailor Jerry Spiced Navy Rum became one of the world's best-selling rums.

All-time sailing records

First around the world, stopping, single-handed:
Joshua Slocum, *Spray*, 1898, 3 years, 2 months, 3 days

First around the world, non-stop, single-handed:
Robin Knox-Johnston (below), *Suhaili*, 1968, 313 days

First around the world, non-stop, single-handed, woman:
Kay Cottee, *First Lady*, 1988, 189 days

First around the world, non-stop, single-handed, 'westabout':
Chay Blyth, *British Steel*, 1971, 292 days

First around the world, non-stop, single-handed, 'westabout', woman:
Dee Caffari, *Aviva*, 2006, 178 days, 3 hours, 5 minutes

Most times around the world, non-stop, single-handed:
Jon Sanders, *Parry Endeavour*, 1988, 657 days (3 continuous circumnavigations)

First transatlantic, single-handed:
Alfred Johnson, *Centennial*, 1876, 46 days

Current sailing records

Round the world, non-stop, crewed:
Loick Peyron, *Banque Populaire*, 2012, 45 days, 13 hours, 42 minutes

Round the world, non-stop, single-handed:
Francis Joyon, *IDEC*, 2008, 57 days, 13 hours, 34 minutes

Round the world, non-stop, single-handed, 'westabout':
JL Van Den Heede, *Adrien*, 2004, 122 days, 14 hours, 3 minutes

Transatlantic, west to east, crewed:
Pascal Bidegorry, *Banque Populaire*, 2009, 3 days, 15 hours, 25 minutes

Transatlantic, west to east, single-handed:
Loick Peyron, *Sodebo*, 2008, 5 days, 19 hours, 30 minutes

Transpacific, west to east, crewed:
Olivier de Kersauson, *Geronimo*, 2006, 13 days, 22 hours, 38 minutes

Transpacific, west to east, single-handed:
Steve Fossett, *Lakota*, 1996, 20 days, 9 hours, 52 minutes

24-hour average speed, crewed:
Pascal Bidegorry, *Banque Populaire*, 2009, 37.8 knots

24-hour average speed, singlehanded:
Francis Joyon, *IDEC*, 2012, 27.75 knots

Source: World Sailing Speed Record Council, www.sailspeedrecords.com

UNITED NATIONS CONVENTION ON THE LAW OF THE SEA, 1982

Article 98: Duty to render assistance
'1. Every State shall require the master of a ship flying its flag, in so far as he can do so without serious danger to the ship, the crew or the passengers:
    (a) to render assistance to any person found at sea in danger of being lost;
    (b) to proceed with all possible speed to the rescue of persons in distress, if informed of their need of assistance, in so far as such action may reasonably be expected of him;
    (c) after a collision, to render assistance to the other ship, its crew and its passengers and, where possible, to inform the other ship of the name of his own ship, its port of registry and the nearest port at which it will call.
2. Every coastal State shall promote the establishment, operation and maintenance of an adequate and effective search and rescue service regarding safety on and over the sea and, where circumstances so require, by way of mutual regional arrangements cooperate with neighbouring States for this purpose.'

YO HO HO...

It's no secret that sailors are fond of a drink – and never more so than when undertaking long, arduous voyages to the far ends of the world. To compensate for their hardships, from the 16th century the Royal Navy rewarded its crews with a daily ration of beer – originally a gallon (4.5 litres) a day. Trouble was, as the British Empire expanded and journeys got longer, the beer tended to go off and the crews became disgruntled. With the colonisation of Jamaica in 1655, the Royal Navy had access to a steady supply of rum and started issuing that instead of beer – half a pint (about one-third of a litre) of

rum replaced a gallon of beer. The ensuing results are not hard to imagine, with drunkenness and lack of discipline being a constant problem. Which is why, on 21 August 1740, Vice Admiral Edward Vernon – known as 'old grog' for his habit of wearing a coat made of a silk-based material called grogam – issued an order that the rum should be diluted with water. The prescribed mixture of his so-called 'grog' was a quart – that is, 2 pints (1.1 litres) – of water to a half-pint of rum, or 4:1 water/rum. Amazingly, the practice of issuing a daily ration of rum to naval ratings continued right up until 1970, when fears over the safety of men operating machinery while under the influence put an end to it. Those darned health and safety regulations!

PASS THE BUCKET – TO LEEWARD

A SEASICK SAILOR sounds like a contradiction – after all, who would willingly go back to sea after suffering the wretched ordeal of seasickness? Yet no less a sailor than Lord Nelson himself was repeatedly seasick throughout his sailing career, and most sailors will admit to having experienced bouts of nausea at sea. The condition is thought to be triggered by a disjunction between the messages being sent to the brain: the eyes say you are stable, because your immediate surroundings are constant, while your inner ear says you are being thrown about all over the place. The result is confusion, followed by nausea, followed by the inevitable yeeeurch!

NATURAL REMEDIES TO CONTROL SEASICKNESS INCLUDE: staying on deck; watching the horizon; eating ginger; drinking cola; not talking; taking the helm; and above all keeping warm, rested and well fed at all times.

WHO GIVES A XXXX FOR JON SANDERS?

Sir Francis Chichester, Sir Chay Blyth, Sir Robin Knox-Johnston, Dame Ellen MacArthur – chances are, if you read a paper and are over 12 years of age, you'll have heard of at least one of these sailors, if not all of them. But what about Jon Sanders? Even most dedicated sailors have probably never heard of him, never mind the general public. Yet, arguably, his achievements outrank his better-known colleagues by a factor of 3:1. Here's why: in 1975–77, Sanders sailed his 34ft (10m) sloop *Perie Banou* (which is the sister ship to former British prime minister, Ted Heath's *Morning Cloud*) around the world to become the first Australian yacht to circumnavigate the world. Not content with that, in 1981–82 he sailed the same boat twice around the world, single-handed and non-stop, clocking up 48,000 miles (77,000km) – half as much again as Knox-Johnston and Blyth did on their respective voyages. Trouble is, Sanders had taken provisions on board in Tasmania and Plymouth, which, according to the World Sailing Speed Record Council, constituted outside assistance and rendered his record null and void. Undaunted by this setback, Sanders got himself a bigger boat, the 46ft (14m) sloop *Parry Endeavour*, and in 1986–88 sailed around the world again: this time he went around three times; the first two times from east to west, and the last time from west to east. The reason for this, in his words, was, 'to break the monotony'. By the time he sailed back to Fremantle, he had been at sea for 657 days and travelled 80,000 miles (129,000km) – non-stop, single-handed and unassisted. But, as I say, you've probably never heard of him. What does it take for an Australian sailor to get noticed?

Olympic records

The Yachting category was created for the first modern Olympics in Athens in 1896, but the event was cancelled due to bad weather. The first sailing event was raced at the 1900 Paris Olympics, where France swept the board, winning all three medals.

The biggest Olympic sailing event was the 1996 Atlanta Olympics, where 436 sailors from 77 countries took part. Hong Kong, Japan, Poland and the Ukraine all won yachting medals for the first time.

The most successful Olympic sailor ever is Britain's Ben Ainslie, who clinched his fourth gold medal at the 2012 London games. He also won silver in 1996, putting him ahead of the previous record holder Paul Elvstrom, who won four golds between 1948 and 1960.

Historically, the sailing event was open to both men and women. A women-only class was introduced at the 1988 Seoul Olympics and was won by Allison Jolley and Lisa Jewel (USA).

Bill and Carl Buchan (USA) became the first father and son to win gold at the same event, when Bill won the Star class and Carl won the Flying Dutchman class at the 1984 Los Angeles Olympics.

Of the 46 classes that have been used for Olympic sailing, the Star is the longest-serving. It made its Olympic debut in 1932 and was raced for the 39th (and probably last) time at the 2012 London Olympics.

NEVER ON FRIGG'S DAY

SAILORS ARE FAMOUSLY a superstitious bunch and, even in this day of GPS and sat nav, there are some who refuse to set sail on a Friday – never mind a Friday 13th. This aversion is thought to originate in Christian mythology. Friday is named after Frigg, the Norse goddess of love and fertility, who was declared a witch by early Christians. Frigg's day was therefore deemed unlucky, and so the superstition spread. There's even an apocryphal story of the Royal Navy commissioning a ship sometime in the 19th century called the HMS *Friday* to disprove the myth – after all, it couldn't afford to have its fleet portbound every Friday! The ship's keel was laid on a Friday, she was launched on a Friday and she was placed under the command of a Captain James Friday. She set sail on her maiden voyage on a Friday, and was never seen again. Needless to say, there is no factual evidence to support this Frigging tale.

TRADING SUGAR FOR SYPHILIS

When Columbus and his crew returned to Europe from the New World, they brought back with them all kinds of delicious new foods: potatoes, tomatoes, corn, cocoa,  pineapples and squash, to name but a few. It's only recently been established that they probably also brought back syphilis. Studies of human skeletons in Europe dating from before Columbus's return show no signs of syphilis – whereas there is evidence of the disease in bones from the New World dating back 7,000 years. The trade in diseases, however, ran overwhelmingly the other way, with the Old World introducing the delights of smallpox, measles, cholera, typhoid, yellow fever and leprosy, to name but a few.

OLDER THAN THE (NEO) OLYMPICS

Contrary to popular belief, the America's Cup is named after a yacht, not the country. In 1851 the schooner *America* came from the New World and beat all comers in a race around the Isle of Wight. The prize was a 100 Guinea Cup put up by the Royal Yacht Squadron, which became known as the America's Cup after its first winner. The New York Yacht Club managed to hang on to the cup for a record 132 years, until 1983, and the America's Cup became the longest continually contested sporting event, beating the modern Olympics by nearly 50 years. Great Britain holds the record for the most unsuccessful challenges, with 19 attempts and no wins. The Scottish-born 'racing grocer' Sir Thomas Lipton made six challenges and, although he never won the Cup, reaped huge financial rewards through his link with the event. The Cup was finally wrested from the NYYC by an Australian challenger in 1983, and since then has been won as many times by non-American teams as American teams.

AMERICA'S CUP SCORE 1851–2010:
USA: 29, New Zealand: 2, Switzerland: 2, Australia: 1, Great Britain: 0, Italy: 0, Canada: 0

'Hunky dory'

Depending on who you believe, this expression is either derived from the name of a street popular among sailors in Yokohama, in Japan, or from the Dutch 'honk', meaning the goal in a game and therefore something desirable, or 'honky'. Certainly there is a street in Yokohama called Honcho Dori, which leads down to the harbour and which may or may not have been the red-light district.

'KISS ME, HARDY' (BUT NOT ON THE LIPS)

IT'S ALWAYS BEEN A SLIGHT EMBARRASSMENT to the Royal Navy that the last words of its greatest ever sailor were to ask a fellow officer to kiss him. Hardly the actions of a hardened fighter, you might think. Or was Nelson just gay? According to three witnesses present at Nelson's death, just before he died at the Battle of Trafalgar in 1805, the English admiral said: 'Take care of my dear Lady Hamilton, Hardy, take care of poor Lady Hamilton.' (Lady Hamilton was his mistress.) He then paused and whispered, 'Kiss me, Hardy.' Hardy kissed him on the forehead, whereupon Nelson said, 'Now I am satisfied. Thank God I have done my duty,' and promptly died. This version of events was never seriously questioned until Victorian times, when it was suggested that perhaps what Nelson had really said was 'Kismet, Hardy,' meaning, 'Fate, Hardy.' In fact, it seems more likely that Georgians were simply less hung up than their Victorian counterparts, and kissing between men wasn't particularly taboo.

WE ARE SAILING

In the old days, it was Humphrey Bogart, Erroll Flynn and Richard Burton who took time out of the limelight to go sailing. Nowadays, going yachting – preferably right in the limelight – is an important part of celebrity culture. Famous/wealthy people photographed on yachts include: Rod Stewart, Tiger Woods, Naomi Campbell, Sting, Orlando Bloom, George Clooney, Cindy Crawford, Bono, Wayne Rooney, David and Victoria Beckham, Leonardo DiCaprio, Bill Gates, Giorgio Armani, Uma Thurman, Brad Pitt and Angelina Jolie, Johnny Depp, Nicholas Cage, Harrison Ford, Ellen DeGeneres, Beyoncé and Jay-Z, Paris Hilton, Richard Branson, Roman Abramovich, Vladimir Putin and (formerly) Saddam Hussein.

KENNEDY THE NAVAL HERO

EVERYONE LOVES A WAR HERO – and none more than the US electorate. When John F Kennedy won the presidency in 1960, he was no doubt helped by events in the Pacific 19 years earlier. In 1941, during World War II, Kennedy was in charge of an 80ft (24m) patrol torpedo boat, when the boat was rammed at night by a Japanese destroyer. Two of the crew were killed and the remaining 11 survivors had to swim 4 miles (6km) to a remote island. Despite suffering a back injury, Kennedy towed a badly burned crewman to safety by clenching a strap from the man's lifebelt between his teeth. The men spent four days avoiding Japanese troops, eventually making contact with Allied forces through local islanders, who carried a message that Kennedy had carved on a coconut shell. He kept the preserved coconut on his desk through his presidency and the story was made into a film.

UNITED NATIONS CONVENTION ON THE LAW OF THE SEA, 1982

Article 99: Prohibition of the transport of slaves
'Every State shall take measures to prevent and punish the transport of slaves in ships authorized to fly its flag and to prevent the unlawful use of its flag for that purpose. Any slave taking refuge on board any ship, whatever its flag, shall ipso facto be free.'

A man who is not afraid of the sea will soon be drowned, [...] for he will be going out on a day he shouldn't. But we do be afraid of the sea, and we do only be drowned now and again.

JM Synge, Irish author (1871–1909)

SEA FOOD

Without the sea, we wouldn't have pizza. Flat bread has been made in eastern Mediterranean countries for centuries, but it was the discovery of the New World that led to the invention of the world's most popular fast food. Italian sailors returning from the Americas brought back tomatoes with them and, once the folks back home realised they weren't poisonous, they were turned into a rich sauce that was spread on the flat bread. In Naples, fishermen's wives gave the new dish to their husbands when they set off in their boats, and thus the Marinara pizza (which doesn't have fish in it) was born.

WHY SAILORS CAN'T SWIM

It is of course a lie that sailors can't swim: most of them can. Back in the 18th century, however, when large numbers of crew were needed to man the mighty square-riggers, sailors came from all sorts of backgrounds and many were even press-ganged into service. Swimming wasn't yet the popular leisure activity it is now, so it's highly likely that most of these men couldn't swim. Neither would they have had much time to learn once they were at sea. It was dangerous to swim from a moving vessel, and they would have had other things to think about while in port. In 1910, a newspaper article estimated that 40 per cent of US Navy conscripts couldn't swim – although the navy was doing everything it could to remedy the situation. However, there was another reason some sailors didn't learn to swim: many figured if they went overboard they wouldn't be rescued anyway. If that was the case, they'd rather die by drowning quickly than spend hours floundering around in the ocean, drowning by slow degrees.

'Son of a gun'

There are several explanations for the origins of this expression, but one of the more interesting is that it originated aboard ship, in the days when wives were allowed to join their menfolk at sea. When a woman gave birth, a section of the gun deck was screened off for the occasion. If the father of the child wasn't known, it would be described in the log as the 'son of a gun' – that is, a bastard. Another explanation is that it is a more generic term for an illegitimate child fathered by military personnel on the move.

JOIN THE CLUB

You might think it's easy enough to work out which is the oldest yacht club in the world. Just look at the records, find out when they were founded, and bob's your boatswain. Trouble is, clubs are by nature competitive and like to come first. Which is why two clubs are currently claiming first place. First up, there's the Neva Yacht Club in St Petersburg, founded in 1718 by Peter the Great. The Tsar even supplied a fleet of sailing ships and designed a club ensign based on the flag of the Russian Navy. Next up, we have the Royal Cork Yacht Club, founded in 1720 by the 9th Lord of Inchiquin, William O'Brien. Although the Neva was formed two years earlier, the Royal Cork points out that the club was originally set up by decree of the tsar rather than as a voluntary association, which is the proper understanding of a yacht club. Who's right? Answers on a postcard…

Ships & shipbuilding

A $630 BILLION INDUSTRY

DESPITE THE PREVALENCE OF LORRIES and trucks on our roads, ships still play a crucial role in keeping our economies working. An astonishing 90 per cent of the world's trade is transported by sea, including everything from cars to bananas. This ocean trade generates some $630 billion in revenue for the companies involved – 5 per cent of global trade, and that's without counting related industries such as finance, insurance and education. And it's not just cargo. Some 19 million passengers are estimated to have taken holidays on cruise ships in 2011, generating more than $29 billion in revenue. Figures for yachting are harder to come by, but the superyacht business alone is thought to be worth around $70 billion.

RETURN OF THE AFRICAN QUEEN

It's one of the most iconic boats in the world and much loved by movie-goers around the world. Yet the *African Queen*, star of the 1951 movie of the same name, languished in a Florida marina for a decade before being spotted by a local couple and restored in 2011. Prior to helping Humphrey Bogart win his only Oscar, it was called the *Livingstone* and was used by the British East Africa Rail Company to carry big-game hunters, missionaries and cargo in the Belgian Congo and Uganda. After its moment of fame, the boat was taken to San Francisco and changed hands several times before ending up in the Florida Keys. Following a £40,000 ($60,000) restoration, it was back in service taking tourists around Key Largo.

NEW AGE OF SAIL

The idea of powering modern cargo ships by sail might seem a little fanciful – after all, cargo-carrying tall ships such as the *Cutty Sark* went out of fashion more than 100 years ago. However, according to the folks at B9 Shipping (part of B9 energy, the UK's biggest wind farm company), it's only a matter of time before oil becomes so scarce and/

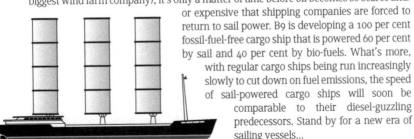

or expensive that shipping companies are forced to return to sail power. B9 is developing a 100 per cent fossil-fuel-free cargo ship that is powered 60 per cent by sail and 40 per cent by bio-fuels. What's more, with regular cargo ships being run increasingly slowly to cut down on fuel emissions, the speed of sail-powered cargo ships will soon be comparable to their diesel-guzzling predecessors. Stand by for a new era of sailing vessels...

WOMEN AND CHILDREN FIRST – BUT ONLY IF THERE'S TIME

Despite its horrific death toll, the evacuation of the *Titanic* in 1912 was on the whole calm and orderly, with women and children being given priority onto the lifeboats – to the extent that many were launched only partially full. This was partly because no one believed the ship was really going to sink and partly because she sank so slowly: passengers and crew had a full 2 hours and 40 minutes to consider their actions. OK, there were more deaths among third class passengers than the other classes, but that reflected the social system of the time which meant the location of their accommodation was in the lower decks.

The scenario on the cruise ship, the *Lusitania*, when she was sunk by a German U-boat three years later couldn't have been more different. Her 1,959 passengers and crew had just 18 minutes to consider their actions. Instead of 'women and children first', it was 'every man for himself', with men and women aged 18–35 most likely to survive. Whereas on the *Titanic*, children were 14.8 per cent *more* likely to survive than men, on the *Lusitania* they were 5.3 per cent *less* likely to survive. And, whereas on the *Titanic*, women were 53 per cent *more* likely to survive than men, on the *Lusitania* they were 1.1 per cent *less* likely to survive.

	RMS *Titanic*	RMS *Lusitania*
Number of lifeboats that could have been carried:	52	n/a
Number of lifeboats actually carried:	20	48
Capacity of lifeboats carried:	1,176	2,605
Number of people on board:	2,223	1,959
Number of people killed:	1,517	1,198
Number of people saved:	706	761
Proportion of men saved:	20 per cent	40 per cent
Proportion of women saved:	74 per cent	38 per cent
Proportion of children saved:	51 per cent	27 per cent
Time taken to sink:	2 hours 40 minutes	18 minutes

AROUND THE SEA IN 84 DAYS

What is the point of a nuclear submarine? Apart from reducing oil consumption, the main benefit of nuclear is that it allows a submarine to remain submerged underwater indefinitely – or at least until the chocolate runs out. And what better way to prove this than to circumnavigate the world underwater? This is exactly what the USS *Triton* did from February to May 1960, becoming the first vessel to do so. The journey was made on her shakedown cruise just three months after she was launched, and followed the same track as Ferdinand Magellan's ship *Victoria*. The actual circumnavigation took 60 days, although the sub was submerged for a total of 84 days. It only emerged to the surface once, to drop off a sick member of the crew in Uruguay. Although the journey was a PR triumph for the USA in the midst of the Cold War, the £38-million ($109-million) *Triton*, with her twin nuclear reactors, proved too expensive to run and was decommissioned in 1969 after only ten years' service.

How to build a lucky boat

❄ Put a coin under the mast.

❄ Don't build hull number 13, because it will be unlucky – although that means hull number 14 is effectively number 13. You have been warned!

❄ Although women are unlucky aboard ship, naked women calm the sea, so carve a figurehead of a naked woman to bring smooth passage.

❄ Paint an eye on the front of the vessel to keep the evil eye away.

THE ORIGINAL *BLACK PEARL*

Although now forever known as the ship sailed by Captain Jack Sparrow in the *Pirates of the Caribbean* movies, the original *Black Pearl* was a more modest, although no less salty, vessel. Under the ownership of Barclay Warburton III, the 52-ft (16-m) topsail schooner took part in the 1972 Tall Ships races in Europe. Inspired by this youth-training event, Warburton founded the American Sail Training Association, with the *Black Pearl* as its flagship. ASTA now has a membership of 250 vessels – most of them many times the size of the *Black Pearl* – and organises Tall Ships races in the Atlantic, the Pacific and the Great Lakes. Under Warburton's ownership, the *Black Pearl* raced in ASTA events for many years, and provided training for some 500 young people. Following Warburton's death in 1983, she went through a succession of owners before ending up in a derelict state in Chester, Connecticut.

MARY CELESTE: WHAT REALLY HAPPENED?

IT's THE STUFF OF FICTION: a ship found in the middle of the Atlantic under full sail, with no crew on board and no sign of a struggle. Yet the story of the *Mary Celeste* is a true tale. Theories about what happened to the ship in 1872 abound, involving ghosts, UFOs, piracy, drunkenness, mutiny, explosions, whirlpools and a seaquake. Even the Vice Admiralty Court of Gibraltar, which conducted a three-month investigation into the case, was unable to reach a firm conclusion. It seems that, for some reason, the crew thought the ship was in peril and abandoned it, taking the ship's papers and navigation equipment with them. The lifeboat they were on became detached from the ship and they either drowned or starved to death. What made them run is the $64,000 question – perhaps the nine empty wine barrels found in the hold are a clue.

OCEAN JUGGERNAUTS

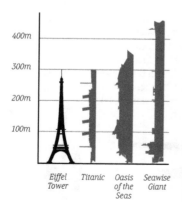

400m
300m
200m
100m

Eiffel Tower   *Titanic*   *Oasis of the Seas*   *Seawise Giant*

The largest ship ever built was the 1,500ft (458m)-long oil tanker *Seawise Giant*. Built in 1979, she was lengthened to her final size before going into service two years later. She was cut up for scrap in 2010. The largest passenger ships ever built were *Oasis of the Seas* and *Allure of the Seas*, both 1,180ft (360m) long and built in 2008 and 2010 respectively. (The *Allure* is said to be 2in (5cm) longer than the *Oasis*, although this may be due to the temperature when measured – heat causing them to lengthen slightly.) The *Oasis* and the *Allure* are each capable of carrying 8,700 passengers and crew – more than double the *Titanic*'s capacity of 3,500. Both ships are longer than the height of the Eiffel Tower – 986ft (300m).

Top boat names

Most popular names in **1991**	Osprey	Windwalker	Miss Behavin'
	Therapy	Obsession	Escapade
	Windsong	Happy Hours	Liquid Asset
	Serenity		
Most popular names in **2011**	Seas the Day	Pegasus	Liquid Asset
	Nauti Buoy	Serenity Now	Miss Behavin'
	Aquaholic	Second Wind	Blew By You
	Dream Weaver		

Source: www.boatus.com

ANCHORS AWEIGH!

IF YOU'VE NEVER OWNED A BOAT, you might be forgiven for thinking there was only one type of anchor. For centuries, sailors managed well enough with the classic Fisherman (or Admiralty Pattern) anchor, as typically depicted on a child's drawing of a boat – although note that the crossbar at the top (called the 'stock') should really be rotated at 180 degrees to the pointy arms at the bottom (the 'flukes'). The trouble with the Fisherman is that it's cumbersome and not easy to store. So, towards the end of the 18th century, a stockless anchor was developed that could be winched up flush against the hull of a ship. But anchor design really took off in the 20th century. First off, in 1933, a British mathematician devised a completely new type of anchor based on a plough. Called the CQR, it's since been widely imitated and is still many sailors' favourite. Another innovation was the Danforth anchor, invented by Richard Danforth in the 1940s for use on landing craft and consisting essentially of two giant flukes hinged to a shaft. Since then, there has been a proliferation of anchors, including the Bruce (a cross between a CQR and a Danforth), the Bulwagga (a Danforth with three flukes), the Rocna (an 'improved' CQR/Bruce) and the Hydrobubble (essentially a small plough fitted with a buoyancy tank). But beware, all sailors have their favourite anchor, and woe betide anyone who tries to tell them another is better.

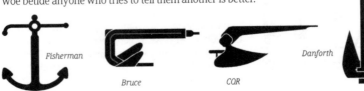

Fisherman   *Bruce*   *CQR*   *Danforth*

FISHY DESIGNS

S hip design, like everything else, follows fashion. Around 200 years ago, the ideal shape for a ship was described as a 'cod's head and mackerel tail' – that is, a bluff bow (front) combined with a fine, streamlined stern (back). The name probably had little to do with any theory of naval architecture, but was simply a handy way of describing the vessels' shape in language that sailors could understand. In the 1930s, symmetrical ends were the order of the day – more of a 'sardine head and sardine tail' – which produced beautiful, elegant boats that sailed in a straight line but weren't particularly fast. Nowadays, yachts are more likely to be the exact opposite of the 18th-century ideal – that is, with a 'mackerel head and cod's tail' – resulting in a hull shape that is fast and performs well to windward. The more extreme designs, such as the Open 60 racers, with their snub bows and flat sterns, might be even described as a 'mullet head and plaice tail'.

THE FLYING DUTCHMAN: TRUTH OR FANTASY?

The tale of a cursed ship doomed to sail around the world endlessly has been told by sailors since the 18th century. Usually the *Flying Dutchman* appears as a mirage in a storm and disappears without trace once approached. Sighting the ship is a sure sign of bad luck and terrible misfortune is meant to follow. According to some, the ship's captain refused to head to port in the face of a terrible storm and was punished for his arrogance; others suggest heinous crimes had been committed by her crew, meaning they could never return to port. Nowadays we know such stories are just crazed visions of homesick sailors who have been at sea for too long, or a strange atmospheric phenomenon. Yet no less a figure than King George V claimed to have seen the ship while sailing off Australia during the 1880s. According to him, 13 people saw the ship, and the first sailor to spot it fell from the fore topmast the next day and died instantly. As recently as the 1940s, the renowned author Nicholas Monsarrat (an ex-Royal Navy Commander) claims to have seen the *Flying Dutchman* in the same part of the Pacific.

Believe me, my young friend, there is nothing – absolutely nothing – half so much worth doing as simply messing about in boats.

The Wind in the Willows by Kenneth Grahame, 1908

Eight major sea battles

Battle of the Nile Delta – Arguably the first naval battle, this took place on the Nile in 1178 BC when the Sea People tried to invade Egypt. Ramesses III lured them into a trap, thereby saving the Egyptian Empire.

Battle of Salamis – A turning point in European history came in 480 BC when 1,200 Persian ships were defeated by 380 Greek ships by the island of Salamis near to Athens in Greece. Ancient Greece was saved, and thereby modern civilisation, too.

Battle of Actium – The tide turned against Mark Antony when his fleet was defeated in the Ionian Sea by Octavian in 31 BC. Octavian became Augustus, and the Roman Republic became the Roman Empire.

Battle of Yamen – Despite being outnumbered 10:1, the invading Yuang Dynasty defeated the Song Dynasty in 1279 and inflicted 100,000 casualties in a mighty sea battle off southern China. The Mongols had arrived.

Battle of Lepanto – A coalition of Catholic forces destroyed the main Ottoman fleet in the Gulf of Patras in 1571, severely stemming further Ottoman expansion in the Mediterranean.

Spanish Armada – King Philip II of Spain's 'Invincible Fleet' proved anything but when 130 ships sailed to England to overthrow Elizabeth I in 1588. After being chased around the British Isles, much of the fleet was shipwrecked in storms off Ireland (below).

Battle of Cartagena de Indias – Another Spain vs England confrontation, this time emphatically won by the Spanish. The Brits lost 50 ships in the battle in 1741 off Colombia, and Spain held sway over South America.

Battle of Trafalgar – Britain's naval supremacy was established when 27 British ships defeated 33 French and Spanish ships off the coast of Spain in 1805. The Franco-Spanish forces lost 20 ships and Britain none – although they did lose Nelson.

DESIGNING THE PERFECT BOAT

THERE ARE MANY RULES OF THUMB for designing a good boat. One of the oldest concerns the ratio of beam to length (that is, width to length). Dinghies are traditionally about 2.5 times as long as they are wide; fishing boats 3:1 and yachts 4–5:1. The longer the boat, the narrower the beam, proportionally speaking. The legendary American designer Howard Chappelle summed it up as follows: 'The most seakindly boats have between three to five beams to their length.' Another old adage says: 'A man needs a foot of boat waterline for every year of his age.' This rule has become outdated, however, as boating has spread to all classes (few people can afford to maintain a 65-footer when they retire) and as the popularity of small-boat cruising has increased. A more appropriate saying for our times is: 'The pleasure you get from sailing is inversely proportional to the size of your boat.' In other words, the smaller the boat, the less work is needed and the more time you have for sailing. Model boats, anyone?

 If a man is to be obsessed by something, I suppose a boat
is as good as anything, perhaps a bit better than most.

EB White, US author (1899–1985)

PLIMSOLL WEATHER

Have you ever noticed the round symbol with a line through it on the side of a cargo ship? It's called a Plimsoll line and shows the maximum amount a ship is allowed to be loaded. If the water rises above the Plimsoll line, it means the ship is overloaded and there's not enough reserve buoyancy. The sign was named after the British MP Samuel Plimsoll, who campaigned to improve safety at sea. It was first introduced in Britain in 1876 but wasn't applied worldwide until 1930. The letters on either side of the circle denote the authority that has inspected the vessel, e.g. LR for Lloyd's Register or BV for Bureau Veritas. Because the buoyancy of water varies depending on temperature and salt content, there are different load lines for a variety of conditions: TF (Tropical Fresh Water), F (Fresh Water), T (Tropical Seawater), WNA (Winter North Atlantic), S (Summer Temperate Seawater) and W (Winter Temperate Seawater).

STARBOARD AND LARBOARD

Why do sailors say port and starboard instead of left and right? Because the side that is left or right will change depending on whether you are facing the front or the back of a ship. Saying left and right aboard ship therefore begs the question: facing which way? That's why sailors always say port (left hand facing forward) and starboard (right hand facing forward). The word starboard is thought to come from the days when ships were steered with an oar or rudder lashed to one side. As the majority of people then, as now, were right-handed, the rudder was usually lashed to the right-hand side. Thus 'star', from the Old Norse *styri* ('rudder'), and 'board' meaning the side of the ship, combined to make starboard, meaning the right-hand side of the ship. The left-hand side was originally called larboard (possibly from 'ladder' – that is, the side moored against the quay with a boarding ladder), but this was too easily confused with starboard and was changed to port in the mid-19th century – possibly because there was a loading port on that side. Confused? Just remember this: 'port' has four letters, same as 'left'. And don't even start on the expression 'port out, starboard home'. That's in the next chapter.

PRESERVED IN ASPIC OF SEA

The raising of the wreck of the *Mary Rose* started in 1979 and was probably the most remarkable feat of underwater archaeology ever. After months of excavation, the hull was hoisted on a purpose-built cradle and brought ashore to Portsmouth, along with nearly 19,000 artefacts – including the remains of her 200 crew. The find offered a unique insight into 16th-century life, which had been perfectly preserved in the silt at the bottom of the Solent. Impressive as that achievement was, the preservation work had only just begun. After being brought to the surface, the timbers had to be sprayed continually to stop them drying out, first with water and, after 1995, with polyethylene glycol. In 2012, the 500-year-old ship was moved into a new £36m museum, where the taps were finally turned off. A four-year process of controlled air-drying has now been started, before the hull can finally be exposed to the atmosphere – more than 500 years after it was built.

MOST POPULAR SAILBOAT EVER?

CALCULATING BOAT SALES is no easy task, as boatbuilders are notoriously bad at keeping track of hull numbers, models change names and production is often subcontracted overseas. The general consensus, however, is that the Catalina 22, a popular American trailer-sailer, is probably the best-selling sailboat ever. First built in California in 1969, the MkI design was in production until 1995, selling more than 15,000 boats. Since then, the MkII and Sport versions have been introduced and these are still in production. It was named 'Trailerable Boat of the Decade' by *Sail* magazine in 1980 and was inaugurated into the Sailboat Hall of Fame in 1995.

Lest we forget

Five most deadly peacetime maritime disasters:

Doña Paz – An estimated 4,300 people were killed when the Philippine ferry collided with an oil tanker en route to Manila in December 1987.

Kiangya – At least 2,750 people died when the Chinese passenger ship hit a mine in the Huangpu River near Shanghai in December 1948.

Le Joola – Nearly 2,000 people were killed when the Senegalese ferry capsized in rough weather off the coast of Gambia in September 2002.

Sultana – Up to 1,800 passengers on the American steamship died when a boiler exploded while on the Mississippi River in April 1865.

Tek Sing – 1,600 were killed when the Chinese junk struck a reef near Indonesia in February 1822.

Five most deadly wartime maritime disasters:

Wilhelm Gustloff – More than 9,000 people were killed when the German ship was sunk by a Soviet submarine while evacuating civilians and Nazi personnel from East Prussia in January 1945.

Goya – About 7,000 people, mostly soldiers, died when the German ship was sunk by a Soviet submarine in the Baltic in April 1945. Only 183 survived.

Armenia – The Soviet hospital ship was bombed by German planes in 1941, killing between 5–8,000. Only eight survived.

Junyō Maru – 4,200 Javanese slave labourers and 2,300 Allied prisoners of war died when the Japanese ship was sunk by a British submarine in September 1944.

Toyama Maru – 5,400 died when the Japanese ship was torpedoed by a US submarine in 1944, igniting fuel barrels in the ship's hold.

OCEAN CLASS HERO

World War II can be seen as a contest between great military machines: HMS *Hood* vs the *Bismarck* on the high seas, and Spitfires vs Messerschmitts in the air. But the job of keeping Europe supplied with food and armaments from the USA fell to the more humble Liberty ships. It all started in 1940, when Britain ordered 60 Ocean class steamers to replace ships sunk by German U-boats. Although the design was anything but pretty, the ship was quick and easy to build and was fitted with coal-powered engines – Britain had plenty of coal. The design was adapted by the USA, mainly replacing the riveted seams with welded construction and fitting an oil-fired engine – the USA had plenty of oil. In 1941–45, some 2,751 Liberty ships were built in 18 shipyards across the USA, the largest number of ships ever built to the same design. At its peak, construction time averaged 42 days, and three Liberty ships were launched every day. The record was four days, 15½ hours from laying the keel to launching.

Day 2   Day 6   Day 14   Day 24

THE DEADLY SUB

What do you do with a weapon that's more deadly to you than your enemy? That was the case with the 40ft (12m) prototype submarine *HL Hunley*, which was built for the US Confederate forces in 1863. Essentially a steel drum with a hand-driven propeller at one end and a barbed torpedo at the other, the *Hunley* was operated by a crew of seven hands and one officer. Unfortunately, the vessel sank twice during training, killing five men the first time and all eight the second time – including its eponymous designer Horace L Hunley. After each

sinking, it was salvaged and put back into operation. The *Hunley* only saw action once, when it successfully impaled a torpedo on the USS *Housatonic*, killing five of its crew members. However, as it headed back to base, it sank yet again, killing eight more crew. So the final score was 21 Confederate vs 5 Union sailors killed. Despite its poor track record, the *Hunley* is said to be responsible for the start of the era of submarine warfare. The vessel was salvaged off Charlestown in 2000 and placed in a tank of fresh water prior to conservation.

THE FULL MONTY

Sails of a full-rigged ship, including starboard studding sails (port studding sails omitted for clarity):

1. Flying jib
2. Jib
3. Fore topmast staysail
4. Fore course
5. Lower fore topsail
6. Upper fore topsail
7. Fore topgallant sail
8. Fore royal
9. Fore skysail
10. Fore lower studding sail
11. Fore topmast studding sail
12. Fore topgallant studding sail
13. Fore royal studding sail

14. Main staysail
15. Main topmast staysail
16. Main topgallant staysail
17. Main royal staysail
18. Main course
19. Lower main topsail
20. Upper main topsail
21. Main topgallant sail
22. Main royal
23. Main skysail
24. Main course studding sail
25. Main topmast studding sail
26. Main topgallant studding sail

27. Main royal studding sail
28. Mizzen staysail
29. Mizzen topmast staysail
30. Mizzen topgallant staysail
31. Mizzen royal staysail
32. Mizzen course, or crossjack
33. Lower mizzen topsail
34. Upper mizzen topsail
35. Mizzen topgallant sail
36. Mizzen royal
37. Mizzen skysail
38. Spanker

WHY IS A BOAT A 'SHE'?

ACCORDING TO NAUTICAL WAGS, a boat is always called 'she' because:

* She needs a lick of paint to keep her looking good.
* She never shows her bottom.
* Once in harbour, she always heads for the buoys.
* She carries her cargo inside her and delivers it safely.
* It takes a good man to handle her.

A more probable (and less sexist!) reason is that sailors have traditionally named their ships after significant women in their families. From there, it would be an easy step to calling the vessel 'she'. One example of this practice was the West-country schooner *Kathleen & May*, which was originally called *Lizzie May*, after the captain's two daughters. When the ship was sold in 1908, the new owner renamed her *Kathleen & May* after his two daughters, and she has been known by this name ever since.

> Ships are the nearest things to dreams that hands have ever made,
> for somewhere deep in their oaken hearts the soul of a song is laid.
>
> Robert N Rose

WHEN IS A ROPE NOT A ROPE?

Every piece of rope you see on a boat has a purpose, be it to hoist a sail, attach a fender or tether the vessel to the pontoon. Once the rope has a designated purpose, it is known as a 'line'. Only the raw material is referred to as 'rope'. Because there are so many lines on a boat (sailing boats especially), most of them have special names, which saves the skipper constantly having to explain which bit of rope they want the crew to pull. These include: halyards (used to hoist the sails up), sheets (used to control the sails once they are hoisted) and painters (used to attach a tender or dinghy). Just to confuse the uninitiated, there are some lines that are also called ropes. These include: bell ropes (used to ring the ship's bell), bolt ropes (used to stiffen the edges of a sail) and foot ropes (used to support a sailor while stowing sail on a Tall Ship). You see, sailors like to keep landlubbers guessing!

Navigation & seamanship

'Aloof'

When sailing close to a lee shore (that is, with the wind blowing *onto* it),
the helmsman might be instructed to hold the ship 'a-luff' – that is, close to
the wind – to prevent it crashing onto the rocks. To be 'a-luff', or aloof,
therefore came to mean keeping your distance.

HOW TO GO TO SEA

GOING TO SEA CAN BE A HAZARDOUS BUSINESS, and a superstitious sailor will go to great lengths not to tempt fate. For a start, don't set sail on a Friday, or on the first Monday in April or the second Monday in August (all have religious connotations). Also, don't set off if you see any of the following before boarding ship: someone with red hair, someone with flat feet, someone who is cross-eyed, a black cat, a black suitcase, a priest or a woman (unless she is naked). When climbing on board, make sure you place your right foot first. Once on the ship, make sure none of the following are on board: pigs, rabbits, flowers, umbrellas, bananas, salmon, priests, of course, and women (unless they are naked). Never say you are sailing to somewhere, just that you are 'headed' somewhere – you might never make it. While at sea, don't whistle, don't ring a wineglass, don't clap your hands, don't throw stones in the sea, don't kill dolphins, seagulls or albatrosses, don't cut your hair, beard or fingernails, and don't count anything – be it fish, cards or the number of miles to your destination. Never say the words 'pig' or 'drown'. And never light a cigarette from a candle, or a sailor will die at sea. Do have tattoos and piercings, do spit into the sea and pour wine on the deck before setting sail, do throw your old shoes overboard, do nail a horseshoe to the mast, and do give birth to a child – although you'll have to manage that without a woman, since they've already been banned (unless they're naked).

 MEN WANTED for hazardous journey. Low wages, bitter cold,
long hours of complete darkness. Safe return doubtful.
Honour and recognition in event of success.

Ernest Shackleton, *The Times, c.* 1900 (probably apocryphal)

SEARCHING FOR THE SEARCHER

The search for a navigable passage north of Canada obsessed many 19th-century explorers – not surprising, given it took ships 140 days to sail from Europe to California. The only thing that obsessed them more was the search for Sir John Franklin's 1845 expedition to find the Northwest Passage. Franklin and 128 crew died after their ships became trapped in ice, and since then more than 40 expeditions have set out to find their remains. It's been said the search for Franklin's lost expedition has done more for Arctic exploration than the search for the Northwest Passage ever did. As for the passage itself, that was discovered by Amundsen in 1905, but has yet to become commercially viable.

WINDY KNOTS

Knots have long been thought to have magical properties, including the power to control the wind. So-called wind-knots were tied into a piece of rope or a rag and sold to superstitious sailors, who would untie the three knots they contained to release the wind. The 17th-century Norwegian poet Petter Dass explained what happened next:

'Untie but the one for a gentle, good breeze,
  The sails will be filled, you make progress with ease;
But if you the second will loosen,
  You pull in the canvas to barely half mast.
The third will send wind that will race you so fast
  That pumps you will have to resort to.'

BEYOND GPS

What could be more reliable than GPS? The answer, strangely enough, is a mountain, a pile of stones or a church tower. These are all features that can be lined up to give a reliable course through a narrow channel or into a harbour. Such transit lines are often described in pilot books or can be plotted on a chart. The leading marks can be existing features of the landscape, such as unusually shaped rocks, or artificial structures, such as brightly painted posts or piles of stones. Either way, they are as fixed and constant as the hazard itself and, unlike GPS, not liable to pack up when splashed by a wave or when the battery runs out. Another GPS-proof method of navigation is to measure the depth of water to track contour lines, particularly where the seabed falls away steeply. As far back as the 4th century BC, Herodotus wrote: 'When you get 11 fathoms and ooze on the lead, you are a day's journey out from Alexandria.'

AROUND THE WORLD IN £130

YOU DON'T NEED MONEY TO SAIL AROUND THE WORLD – that's the lesson of Evgeny Gvozdev's epic three-year voyage. The 70-year-old Russian sailor couldn't afford to buy a boat so he decided to build one – not in his back garden like many aspiring sailors, but on the balcony of his tiny upstairs flat in Makhachkala, by the Caspian Sea. Built from whatever scraps he could get his hands on, the 11.8ft (3.6m) *Said* ('friend' in Arabic) cost him £130. When the boat was finished, he lowered it into the back of a friend's truck and drove it down to the sea. He set off around the world in 1999, making a complete circumnavigation via Chile, Tahiti, Australia and India, arriving in the Ukraine in 2003. He had no phone, no radio and GPS, and navigated using a plastic sextant, a compass and charts he traded for en route. Sadly, his luck ran out on a subsequent voyage in 2008, when he was found dead on a beach in southern Italy, not far from his stranded yacht.

VANISHING POINT

The story of the Bermuda Triangle (also known as the Devil's Triangle) started in 1945 when five US Navy aircraft, known as Flight 19, set off from Fort Lauderdale in Florida on a routine patrol. A few hours later, the aircraft reported their compasses were not working and 'nothing seem[ed] right'. Soon after, they vanished without trace. The story was subsequently taken up by journalists who identified an area

between Bermuda, Puerto Rico and Miami, where they claimed numerous aircraft and ships had inexplicably disappeared. Since then, the theory has been reported by other writers, with hundreds of cases of missing boats reported in the area. A variety of causes are blamed, including unusual geological conditions, rogue waves, giant methane bubbles, influences from the lost continent of Atlantis and UFOs. Both the US Coast Guard and Lloyd's of London, however, deny that an unusual number of craft have been lost in the area. But then they would, wouldn't they? Because, as every conspiracy theorist knows, they are part of the conspiracy.

Some missing ships from the Bermuda Triangle

USS *Cyclops* – US Navy supply ship, vanished in 1918 with 306 passengers and crew.

Cotopaxi – Tramp steamer, vanished in 1925 (32 crew).

Suduffco – Tramp steamer, vanished in 1926 (29 crew).

Anglo Australian – Tramp steamer, vanished in 1938 (38 crew).

USS *Proteus* – Sister ship of *Cyclops* (above), vanished in 1941.

USS *Nereus* – Another sister ship of *Cyclops* (above), also vanished in 1941.

Samkey – Tramp steamer, vanished in 1948 (43 crew).

Sandra – Tramp steamer, vanished in 1950 (12 crew).

Southern Districts – Freighter, vanished in 1954 (12 crew).

Marine Sulphur Queen – Tanker, vanished in 1963 (39 crew).

Sylvia L Ossa – Freighter, vanished in 1976 (37 crew).

Poet – Freighter, vanished in 1980 (34 crew).

Jamanic K – Freighter, vanished in 1995.

Genesis – Freighter, vanished in 1998.

JAPAN'S DEVIL SEA

On the other side of the world from the Bermuda Triangle exists another area of sea where ships and planes disappear never to be seen again, electronic equipment malfunctions and there have been sightings of ghost ships and UFOs. Welcome to the Dragon's Triangle, Japan's very own sea of mystery, located about 60 miles (100km) south of Tokyo. Some claim dragons live beneath the sea and churn up storms with their tails. It is certainly an area of great seismic activity, where islands appear and then disappear as a result of volcanic eruptions. A few might even erupt unexpectedly, causing sudden waves and sending up great spouts of molten lava – enough to give a very convincing impression of a dragon.

> ❝ Many men have seen [UFOs] and have not been mistaken. Who are we to doubt their word? Only a few weeks ago a Palermo policeman photographed one, and four Italian Navy officers saw a 300ft long fiery craft rising from the sea and disappearing into the sky. Why should these men of law enforcement and defence lie? ❞
>
> Lord Rankeillour, speaking in the British House of Lords, 1979

TEN TIPS FOR SURVIVAL AT SEA

❀ Relax. Taking it easy conserves your energy and minimises the need for food.

❀ Collect rainwater and dew in any available containers.

❀ Fish at night, using a torch to attract the fish.

❀ Small fish can be eaten whole or used as bait. Keep the internal organs of bigger fish for bait.

❀ Suck the eyeballs and bones of fish to extract moisture.

❀ Dry any surplus fish in the sun to eat later.

❀ Protein such as fish makes you thirsty. Don't eat it unless you have drinking water.

❀ Seabirds are a good source of nutrients and are sometimes easier to catch than fish. Skin them rather than plucking them, and eat them cooked or raw.

❀ Plankton is very nutritious and easy to catch by trailing a net or any item of clothing in the sea. Eat two spoonfuls a day.

❀ Seaweed is usually abundant and can contain up to 25 per cent protein and 50 per cent carbohydrates. It is also a laxative, so should only be consumed in moderation.

Source: *Crisis Times*

TO DRINK OR NOT TO DRINK...

'Water, water, every where, nor any drop to drink.'

THUS SPOKE COLERIDGE'S ANCIENT MARINER, and it's a refrain that must haunt anyone unfortunate enough to find themselves stuck in a liferaft with no fresh water, surrounded by sea and slowly dying of thirst. For the advice for many centuries has been: *Don't drink seawater. It will make you even more thirsty and drive you crazy.* One man decided to question that wisdom. In 1952, Alain Bombard crossed the Atlantic in an inflatable dinghy with no food. Instead, he fed himself by eating two spoonfuls of plankton per day, consuming the juices of fish he caught and crushed, and drinking seawater. When he arrived in Barbados after 65 days at sea, he had lost 55lb (25kg) in weight, was anaemic and had lost all his toenails. But he had proved his point: drinking salt water in small quantities doesn't make you go crazy and can help you survive. If only the Ancient Mariner had known...

 The sea finds out everything you did wrong.

Francis Stokes, trans-oceanic sailor (1926–2008)

TOO POSH TO BE TRUE

IT CERTAINLY MAKES A GREAT YARN. According to popular mythology, the word 'posh' came from the days of the Raj, when P&O liners ferried thousands of passengers between the UK and India. According to the story, the cabins on the port (that is, left) side of the ships faced away from the sun on the way to India and were therefore cooler, while the cabins on the starboard (that is, right) side were cooler on the way back to the UK. More affluent passengers therefore always sailed 'port out, starboard home', hence the acronym POSH. Some versions even claim POSH was stamped on certain tickets, or scrawled on luggage in chalk. Needless to say, no such inscribed tickets or luggage have

survived. Indeed, most language experts agree that acronyms were rarely if ever used before the 20th century – the term 'acronym' itself only being coined in the 1940s. A more likely source is from a satirical series published in *Punch* from 1888 that includes a character called Murray Posh, who was indeed a 'swell' and would have bagged himself the best cabin on any ship.

THE PROBLEM OF LONGITUDE

Latitude and longitude are what sailors use to determine their position at sea. You can work out your latitude quite easily by measuring the height of the sun or a star with a sextant and referencing the angle with a set of tables at the corresponding time. Longitude is more difficult to work out. As the world turns on its axis, the midday sun moves along the lines of longitude, which creates different time zones. For every 15 degrees you go to the west, the local time is one hour earlier, while for every 15 degrees you go to the east, the local time is one hour later. This means that, if you can work out the time difference between where you are and a known point such as Greenwich (which is 0 degrees), you can work out your longitude. The trouble was, no one had a clock reliable enough to keep the time with that degree of accuracy.

This is why in 1714 the British government decided to offer a £20,000 prize for a simple method of calculating longitude within 30 miles (50km). All kinds of crazy schemes were suggested, but all were either too complicated or too inaccurate until John Harrison invented a series of clocks so accurate that ships could sail for years on end and still know the time at Greenwich. Although he had solved the problem of longitude, it took him the rest of his life to persuade the British government to award him the prize money, and he was nearly 80 before he finally received official recognition and full payment.

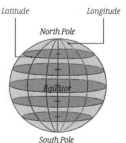

Latitude *Longitude*
North Pole
Equator
South Pole

TOP TEN KNOTS

The *Ashley Book of Knots* may contain 3,000-plus knots, but the truth is that most tasks on a boat can be achieved using less than ten knots. Which are they? Well, you could start with these:

BOWLINE – A fantastically versatile knot that gets stronger the harder it is pulled and yet it can still always be 'broken' (that is, untied).

SHEET BEND – A deceptively simple way of tying two ropes together, especially when one is thicker than the other.

CLOVE HITCH – The 'instant' knot, quick to learn and quick to tie, although there are more reliable knots for the long term.

ROUND TURN AND TWO HALF HITCHES – The workhorse; not as glamorous as the others, but gets you out of trouble time and time again.

REEF KNOT – A perfect, pleasingly symmetrical binding knot, so-called because it's used to reduce, or reef, sails in windy weather.

FISHERMAN'S KNOT – A reliable hitch for slippery lines, quicker and more stylish than the round turn and two half hitches knot.

ZEPPELIN BEND – A relatively little-known gem for tying two ropes together. As its name suggests, it was originally devised to tether Zeppelins.

CONSTRICTOR KNOT – Another binding knot, but this time one that won't come undone, ever. Keep a knife handy to release the rope.

FIGURE OF EIGHT – The stopper knot; prevents ropes pulling through apertures without becoming impossible to untie.

CLEAT HITCH – The ubiquitous mooring-line knot. Despite its popularity, it's nearly always wrongly tied. Come on boaters – you can do better!

'MAYDAY'

The emergency call 'MAYDAY' originates from the French *m'aidez* ('help me') and should be repeated three times in a row to signal a life-threatening situation. Making a false MAYDAY call is a criminal offence in the USA, punished by up to six years in prison and a $250,000 fine.

HOW TO TIE A BOWLINE WITH A RABBIT

Make a loop or 'hole' about 2ft (60cm) from the end of the rope. Imagine the end of the rope is a rabbit and the long end of the rope is a tree. The rabbit jumps upwards out of the hole, runs around the tree, and then jumps back down the hole. Hold the tree and pull the two strands in the hole to tighten.

'PAN PAN'

A lower level emergency call than MAYDAY, derived from the French panne ('breakdown').
Like a MAYDAY, the word is repeated three times, followed by the nature of the emergency.

HOW DOES A COMPASS WORK?

MAGNETIC COMPASSES WORK on the same principle as all magnets: the attraction of opposites. Imagine the Earth is a giant magnet, with two poles: north (negative) and south (positive). Place another magnet against it and it will automatically try to line up its positive with the Earth's negative, and vice versa. That's exactly what's happening inside a compass: the magnetic needle inside is determined to line itself up with the Earth's magnetic field, with its negative end pointing to north and positive end pointing south. Just to make things more difficult, the magnetic north and south poles don't line up exactly with the 'true' north and south used on maps. The difference between the true bearing and the magnetic one is called variation and varies depending where you are. The presence of large metal objects on a ship, such as an engine, also exerts a magnetic influence on a compass, which is called deviation. Sailors have to take into account both variation and deviation before they can work what course to steer on a ship's compass. And that's not to mention trying to predict the influence of wind and currents…

North

Magnetic axis

South

WHO NEEDS A COMPASS?

Long before Captain Cook started charting the Pacific, the Polynesians were navigating the ocean without the use of instruments or charts. They had learned to 'read' the elements. The waves built up by the prevailing winds could be relied on to 'set' in the same direction. A build-up of clouds usually meant there was land beneath, and even at night a slight glow on the horizon suggested there must be an island thereabouts. Perhaps most impressively, without ever resorting to a sextant, they navigated by the stars. By memorising the position of the constellations, they crossed vast tracts of oceans with a confidence that can only be envied by most modern sailors. Likewise, the sailors of northern Europe studied the habits of birds to show them the direction of land. If an auk flew past a Viking boat with a beak full of fish, they knew it was heading back to its nest. If its beak was empty, then it would be heading out to sea to fill it.

GPS'S DELIBERATE MISTAKE

You might think the goal of anyone providing GPS (Global Positioning System) signals is to provide maximum accuracy. Not according to the US military. Originally developed as a means of locating targets and guiding missiles, GPS only became available to civilians as the result of a directive by President Reagan that it should be developed for 'the common good'. But the US military didn't like the idea of its enemies being able to use the system with the same level of accuracy that it could, so it introduced a deliberate error into the signal, thereby reducing its accuracy from 65ft (20m) to 325ft (100m). Selective Availability (SA), as the scrambling technique was called, was implemented in March 1990 and applied to all civilian GPS – including commercial shipping, aircraft, and so on. Only authorised (that is, military) users were provided with encrypted machines that could bypass it. Eventually, a parallel system was developed by GPS manufacturers that largely bypassed SA, and by then it had become apparent that US forces themselves were increasingly using civilian instruments and therefore suffering from the effects of SA. So, in May 2000, President Clinton ordered it to be turned off. At a stroke, the accuracy of GPS was improved by tenfold.

MEASURING SPEED

Long before the advent of modern instrumentation, sailors devised an easy way to measure the speed of their vessel. At its simplest, it consisted of tying a log to a piece of rope, throwing the log in the water and then measuring how much rope ran out over a set period of time. This gave you the distance travelled over water during that time, from which you could work out your speed. Things got a bit more sophisticated with the introduction of the chip log in the 15–16th century. This was essentially a flat piece of wood that was weighted with lead on one side and attached to a bridle to keep it upright in the water. The log was attached to a line with knots tied every 42ft (12.8m). As the log was lowered into the water, a 30-second sandglass was turned, and the line was paid out. The number of knots released during the 30 seconds gave the speed in nautical miles per hour – or knots. As the definition of a nautical mile was refined, the space between knots was changed to 47ft 3in (14.4m) and the sandglass turning changed to 28 seconds. The chip log was eventually replaced by a spinning rotor. This was then replaced by an impeller, which was finally replaced by ultrasonic sensors – but the instrument used for measuring a ship's speed is still called the log, and the unit of measurement is still the knot.

MARVIN CREAMER'S EXTRAORDINARY VOYAGE

ON 21 DECEMBER 1982 a quietly spoken professor of geography set off to sail around the world without the use of navigation instruments. Marvin Creamer was determined to prove that, simply by observing nature, modern humans could navigate the oceans just as the ancients had done. Wave shapes, the colour of the sea, cloud formations and even drifting flotsam yielded valuable data. At one point, he worked out his course by the squeaking of a hatch, deducing that it was caused by dry air currents coming off the Antarctic. Creamer and his crew returned to Cape May on 13 May 1984, after 510 days at sea, having anticipated their landfall by the landing of a housefly on their boat.

ATLANTIC ROUTES: FAST 'N' ICY OR SLOW 'N' SUNNY?

It's a long way across the Atlantic, so you'd assume anyone sailing from Europe to America would take the shortest route possible. That route would take you north, up towards Iceland, fetching up in Newfoundland some 2,000 miles (3,200km) later. Trouble is, this route puts you on a collision course with an almost continuous string of storms generated by the Azores high. That's why most sailors heed the age-old advice to 'head south until the butter melts, and then turn right'. The southern route, crossing via the Canaries to the Caribbean, adds nearly 1,000 miles (1,600km) but makes the most of the trade winds and may actually be faster. An alternative is the so-called middle or intermediate route, which takes you via the Azores and Bermuda, avoiding the worst of the storms. Your butter may not melt, but you're also less likely to starve to death on the way.

DAVID VS GOLIATH

This is a 'true story' that's been doing the rounds for years and has a classic David-and-Goliath appeal. Who your David and Goliath are depend on where your sympathies lie. Most versions feature Americans vs Canadians, although sometimes it's British vs Irish. The details can be adjusted to suit your prejudice.

AMERICANS: Please divert your course 15 degrees to the north to avoid a collision.

CANADIANS: Negative. Please divert your course 15 degrees to the south to avoid a collision.

AMERICANS: This is the captain of a US Navy ship. I say again, divert YOUR course.

CANADIANS: No. I say again, you divert YOUR course.

AMERICANS: This is an aircraft carrier, the second-largest ship in the American Atlantic fleet. We are accompanied by three destroyers, three cruisers and numerous support vessels. I demand that YOU change your course 15 degrees north or countermeasures will be undertaken to ensure the safety of this ship.

CANADIANS: This is a lighthouse. Your call.

LAND MILES VS NAUTICAL MILES

A NAUTICAL MILE IS DIRECTLY LINKED to the shape of the Earth. Imagine the circle formed at the Equator (or any other Great Circle line), and divide that into 360 degrees. Then divide each degree into 60 minutes. Each of those minutes is worth one mile. This makes it very easy for sailors to measure distances on charts, as the minutes of latitude are marked on scales on either side of a chart. By using a pair of dividers, they can measure the distance straight off the chart, without having to make any calculations. Since 1929, a nautical mile has been fixed at exactly 6,076ft (1,852m). A land mile (also called a statute mile) has completely different origins and is about 5,278ft (1,609m).

CHARTING THE UNKNOWN

There's little doubt that Captain Cook deserved his epitaph as 'the ablest and most renowned navigator this or any other country has produced'. Although many of the lands he visited had already been discovered by previous explorers, he measured and recorded their exact shapes and drew the first accurate maps of the South Pacific. Out of confusion, he created order. The charts he produced during his three trips to Australasia on HMS *Endeavour* and HMS *Resolution* – mostly using ordinary navigation instruments such as quadrants, sextants and compasses – were so accurate that they still formed the basis of modern charts well into the 20th century. And he was a fast worker, charting the 2,400 miles (3,900km) of the New Zealand coast in six months, and another 2,000 miles (3,200km) of Australian coast in four months. Cook did make mistakes, however, such as thinking the Banks Peninsula on South Island was an island and that Stewart Island was a peninsula, and not realising Tasmania was an independent island in its own right.

COOK'S THREE VOYAGES:
* First voyage, on HMS *Endeavour* 1768–71
* Second voyage, on HMS *Resolution* 1772–75
* Third voyage, on HMS *Resolution* 1776–79

DING! DING!

Imagine you are sailing off the White Cliffs of Dover in fog. Your sat nav has broken down, and you need to know how far it is to land. What to do? The solution is to ring the ship's bell and time how long it takes for you to hear the echo. Since sound travels at a speed of 1,082ft (330m) per second, the distance to shore and back will be 1,082ft for every second. So if it takes 3 seconds, it must be 3 x 1,082ft – that is, 3,246ft (989m) there and back. Divide by two, and you've got your distance from the shore – that is, 1,623ft (495m). Simple when you know how.

Pirates & smugglers

In an honest service there is thin commons, low wages, and hard labour; in this, plenty and satiety, pleasure and ease, liberty and power; and who would not balance creditor on this side, when all the hazard that is run for it, at worst, is only a sour look or two at choking [that is, hanging]. No, a merry life and a short one, shall be my motto.

Bartholomew Roberts, aka 'Black Bart'

UNITED NATIONS CONVENTION ON THE LAW OF THE SEA, 1982

Article 101: Definition of piracy
'(a) Any illegal acts of violence or detention, or any act of depredation, committed for private ends by the crew or the passengers of a private ship or a private aircraft, and directed:

    (i) on the high seas, against another ship or aircraft, or against persons or property on board such ship or aircraft;
    (ii) against a ship, aircraft, persons or property in a place outside the jurisdiction of any State;
(b) any act of voluntary participation in the operation of a ship or of an aircraft with knowledge of facts making it a pirate ship or aircraft;
(c) any act of inciting or of intentionally facilitating an act described in subparagraph (a) or (b). [...]

Article 103: Definition of a pirate ship or aircraft
A ship or aircraft is considered a pirate ship or aircraft if it is intended by the persons in dominant control to be used for the purpose of committing one of the acts referred to in article 101. The same applies if the ship or aircraft has been used to commit any such act, so long as it remains under the control of the persons guilty of that act. [...]

Article 105: Seizure of a pirate ship or aircraft
On the high seas, or in any other place outside the jurisdiction of any State, every State may seize a pirate ship or aircraft, or a ship or aircraft taken by piracy and under the control of pirates, and arrest the persons and seize the property on board.

Article 107: Ships and aircraft which are entitled to seize on account of piracy
A seizure on account of piracy may be carried out only by warships or military aircraft, or other ships or aircraft clearly marked and identifiable as being on government service and authorized to that effect.'

THE TEN BADDEST PIRATES

EDWARD LOW – One of the most sadistic pirates on the high seas, Low is said to have cut the lips off one of his captives, cooked them and forced the man to eat them. He attacked hundreds of ships in 1722–24 and massacred many of his victims. His final fate is uncertain.

CHEUNG PO TSAI – Although relatively unknown in the West, Po Tsai is arguably the most successful pirate in history, at his peak commanding 20,000 men and several hundred ships. Rumours persist of his hidden treasure.

FRANÇOIS L'OLONNAIS – They don't get much meaner than this French pirate, who regularly dished out torture and beheadings. He met a suitably violent end at the hands of a Panamanian tribe, whose members are said to have chopped him up into small pieces and then ate him for dinner.

EDWARD TEACH, AKA 'BLACKBEARD' – Probably the most famous pirate ever, this former British privateer was the scourge of the eastern Caribbean in 1716–18. He is said to have put wicks in his hair, which he lit during battle to scare his opponents. It took more than five gunshots and 20 knife wounds to kill him.

CHARLES VANE – Another sadist, who treated his crew almost as badly as his enemies, Vane refused the King's Pardon and survived a mutiny before being captured and hanged in Jamaica in 1721.

FRANCIS DRAKE – Although regarded as a national hero in Britain for being the first Briton to sail around the world, Francis Drake made his fortune preying on Spanish ships carrying gold and silver from South America (right).

DANIEL MONTBARS – Known as 'Montbars the Exterminator', the French pirate liked nothing better than torturing his victims. One of his tricks was to cut open a victim's stomach, nail his intestines to a post and make him dance to his death.

BARTHOLOMEW ROBERTS – In less than four years of pirating, this Welsh pirate, also known as 'Black Bart', captured 400 ships. His violent death in 1722 and the hanging of most of his crew is said to have ended the golden age of piracy.

HAYREDDIN BARBAROSSA – This pirate started his career in the Mediterranean attacking Christian ships, particularly the Spanish. He later invaded Algiers and, with the help of the Ottoman Empire, resisted Spanish expansion eastwards.

BENJAMIN HORNIGOLD – The man who gave Blackbeard his first pirate command accepted the King's Pardon in 1718 and promptly turned pirate-hunter. He never caught his main target Charles Vane, and died when his ship struck a reef off Mexico in 1719.

THE FIVE BADDEST WOMEN PIRATES

CHING SHIH – A former prostitute, Shih took over a fleet of 50,000 pirates after her husband died in 1807. Although she behaved brutally towards her victims, including beheading hundreds of them, she insisted on a strict code of conduct – for example, execution was the punishment for any pirate who raped female captives.

GRACE O'MALLEY – Grace led a notorious clan of pirates who preyed on passing ships off the west coast of Ireland, offering safe passage in return for payment. She was eventually captured by the British but reached an agreement with Queen Elizabeth I and returned to Ireland to become a folk hero.

ANNE BONNY – When her first pirate husband turned informant, Bonny, who wanted to be a real pirate, hooked up with John 'Calico Jack' Rackham instead. They were later joined by Mary Read (below). All three were captured and sentenced to death in 1720, but both Bonny and Read managed to escape the noose by claiming that they were pregnant.

MARY READ – Raised as a boy, Read served in the army as a man before leaving to marry a fellow-soldier. When her husband died, she went to sea and became a pirate after the ship she was on was captured by John Rackham. She and Anne Bonny were rumoured to be lovers, though the pair claimed they were only friends. Mary died in prison in Jamaica in 1720.

CHARLOTTE DE BERRY – After being kidnapped and forced to go to sea, Charlotte de Berry organised a mutiny and killed her abductor. A life of piracy followed that was punctuated by episodes of great cruelty.

THE OTHER BLACK PEARL

'The *Black Pearl* is moderately armed, she carries 32 twelve-pound cannons: 18 on the gun deck and 14 on the upper deck. Its full broadside contains 16 cannonballs and weighs 192lb (87kg). Strangely, the *Pearl* has no bow chasers or stern chasers (cannons used while being chased or chasing, as one cannot use a regular broadside volley in this situation), which is very unusual for a pirate ship, giving her a grave tactical disadvantage during a chase; the *Pearl* isn't able to shoot the ship she chases or to reply her hunter's fire. Her high speed only partially negates this handicap. […] She flies a jib, fore staysail, foresail, fore topsail, fore topgallant sail, mainsail, topsail, topgallant sail, mizzen lateen sail, mizzen topsail, main staysail, topmast staysail, topgallant staysail. It's unknown if she has studding sails.'

Source: www.theblack-pearl.com/Black%20Pearl.html

'Avast'

Although now completely associated with 'pirate talk', avast is an archaic nautical term meaning to stop or desist from doing something. It is thought to originate from the Dutch phrase *houd vast* ('hold fast').

21ST-CENTURY PIRATES

Modern pirates may not have wooden legs or parrots on their shoulders, but they are every bit as dangerous as the pirates of old. Most of them operate from fast speedboats and attack cargo ships with guns, torpedoes and rocket-propelled grenades. Their targets are the ship's equipment and any cash held on board, but increasingly they hijack the ship itself and hold it to ransom. According to the International Maritime Bureau, 439 ships were attacked in 2011, of which 45 were hijacked and more than 800 crew taken as hostage. Eight crew were killed. The most dangerous area is the coast of Somalia and the Red Sea, where 236 attacks took place. So successful have they been that the US Navy has led an international effort to crack down on their activities, with at least 20 base ships captured in 2011 alone. Despite these efforts, as of mid-2012, Somalian pirates were holding 11 ships and 174 crew to ransom.

TOP 12 MODERN SMUGGLERS

THE GOODS AND METHODS MAY HAVE CHANGED, but smuggling is still big business. Guns and drugs are the favourite goods, and container ships flying flags of convenience are the favourite method. The countries owning the most ships reported for smuggling are listed below, along with their share of that total, with their global merchant shipping totals in brackets. All things being equal, the two figures should be about the same, but several countries show a severe imbalance.

GERMANY – 19.5 per cent (7.1 per cent)
GREECE – 10.6 per cent (8.2 per cent)
USA – 7.8 per cent (4.3 per cent)
NORTH KOREA – 4.8 per cent
(0.1 per cent)
PANAMA – 4.3 per cent (0.1 per cent)
IRAN – 3 per cent (0.5 per cent)

NORWAY – 2.4 per cent (4.6 per cent)
RUSSIA – 2.4 per cent (6 per cent)
BELIZE – 1.9 per cent (0.01 per cent)
NETHERLANDS – 1.9 per cent (2 per cent)
DENMARK – 1.7 per cent (2 per cent)
JAPAN – 1.7 per cent (8.4 per cent)

Source: Stockholm International Peace Research Institute (SIPRI)

MALACCA MAYHEM

THE STRAIT OF MALACCA has long been a vital trade artery between the Indian and Pacific Oceans, linking countries such as India, China, Japan and South Korea. This convergence of wealth, packed into a stretch of water less than 3 miles (5km) wide at its narrowest point, has also made the Strait a natural target for pirates. The problem exploded in the 18th and 19th centuries, with the arrival of European traders, making the Strait of Malacca one of the most feared navigational areas in the world. The Strait still plays an important part in modern trade, with more than 50,000 ships passing through it every year. And piracy was, until very recently, rife. The International Maritime Bureau reported 220 attacks in the strait in 2000, including a suicide bombing by al-Qaeda that killed 17 US sailors. In 2004, however, the Malacca Straits Patrol was formed to eradicate the problem, and only one incident was reported there in 2011.

CHECK YOUR FLAG

Of the 439 ships attacked by pirates in 2011, these were the most popular targets:

Flag
PANAMA – 71 attacks
LIBERIA – 57 attacks
MARSHALL ISLANDS – 45 attacks
SINGAPORE – 32 attacks
MALTA – 25 attacks
HONG KONG – 21 attacks
ANTIGUA AND BARBUDA – 16 attacks
MALAYSIA – 14 attacks

Country of ownership
SINGAPORE – 65 attacks
GERMANY – 64 attacks
GREECE – 58 attacks
HONG KONG – 27 attacks
JAPAN – 19 attacks
MALAYSIA – 17 attacks
INDIA – 14 attacks
UAE/UK/CHINA/DENMARK – 12 attacks each

Source: International Maritime Bureau

'Shiver me timbers'

An exclamation of surprise. There's little agreement on the expression's origins, but it seems likely it relates to a ship's timbers shuddering in a storm. Since the timbers are the equivalent of a ship's skeleton, it might also refer to someone's bones rattling with fear – a true piratical explanation. The expression was popularised by Long John Silver in *Treasure Island*, who used it seven times, and revived by the singer Tom Waits with his song 'Shiver Me Timbers'.

THE POWER OF PROHIBITION

THE YEARS OF PROHIBITION (1920–33) in the USA were a boom time for American smugglers. As the law only applied to territorial waters 3 miles (5km) off the US coast, it was perfectly legal for ships to moor up outside that boundary with their holds full of booze that smaller, faster boats would then ferry to shore. At its peak, there were dozens of vessels moored off New Jersey on what became known as Rum Row. Some offered their customers on-board entertainment, including prostitutes. At first, the drink of choice was Caribbean rum, leading to the term rum-runners, but the smugglers soon realised they could increase their profit by carrying more expensive liquors, such as whisky, gin and champagne from Canada and Europe. But, unsurprisingly, it

wasn't all happy partying. There was a great deal of competition between smugglers who weren't adverse to looting each others' ships rather than sailing back to distant ports for fresh supplies. When the territorial limit was increased to 12 miles (19km), bigger craft were needed to act as mother ships, which meant the run back to land became riskier. The price of smuggled booze went up, and the profits for those who carried on with the trade went up correspondingly.

THE REAL MCCOY?

The most famous Prohibition rum-runner was a larger-than-life character called William McCoy – a teetotaller. William and his brother Ben turned to smuggling when their Florida boatbuilding business dried up. Spotting an opportunity, they sold up and bought the 90ft (27m) schooner *Henry L Marshall*, which they filled with booze from the Bahamas and moored off the coast of Georgia, USA. So profitable was the trade that they soon upgraded to the 130ft (40m) schooner *Tomoka*, which made several trips to Rum Row during 1922 to 1923. Despite the quasi-illegal nature of his business, McCoy acquired a reputation for straight dealing, never 'cutting' his alcohol with water and refusing to go into cahoots with the criminal gangs that came to dominate the trade. Some claim this is the source of the expression 'the real McCoy', although this is disputed. McCoy and his ship were captured by the US Coast Guard off New Jersey in November 1923, in questionable circumstances, and he was imprisoned for nine months. After serving his term, he invested in real estate and is said to have become an accomplished painter.

THE PIRATES' CODE OF CONDUCT

- Every man has a vote in affairs of moment.
- Every man has equal title to fresh provisions or strong liquors at any time seized, and may use them at pleasure unless a scarcity make it necessary for the good of all to vote a retrenchment.
- If any man defrauds the Company to the value of a dollar, in plate, jewels or money, he shall be marooned.
- If any man defrauds another man, his ears and nose shall be split and he shall be set on shore somewhere he is sure to encounter hardships.
- No person to game at cards or dice for money.
- The lights and candles to be put out at eight o'clock at night. If any of the crew after that hour remain inclined to drinking, they shall do so on the open deck.
- To keep their piece, pistol and cutlass clean and fit for service.
- No boy or woman to be allowed aboard ship. If any man is found seducing any of the latter sex and carrying her to sea disguised, he shall suffer Death.
- Any man who deserts the ship or their quarters in battle shall be punished with Death or Marooning.
- No striking one another on board, but every man's quarrel to be ended on shore, at sword and pistol.
- No man to talk of breaking up this way of living till each has a share of £1,000.
- If any man should lose a limb or become a cripple in their service, he shall have £200 out of the public stock, and for lesser hurts proportionally.
- The captain and quartermaster to receive two shares of a prize; the master, boatswain and gunner, one share and a half; and the other officers one and a quarter.
- The musicians to have rest of the Sabbath day, but the other six days and night none, without special favour.

Based on 'The Articles of Bartholomew Roberts', as detailed in *A General History of the Robberies and Murders of the Most Notorious Pyrates* by Captain Charles Johnson, published 1724

FOUNDING SMUGGLER

Smugglers have a long tradition in the USA, where they are regarded by some as the ultimate free-traders. Indeed, one of the Founding Fathers was the wealthy trader John Hancock, who defied British taxes by smuggling goods such as tea and molasses in his fleet of ships. Hancock was one of the instigators of the Boston Tea Party and his ostentatious signature tops the list of names on the original Declaration of Independence.

THE KING OF PRUSSIA

John Carter wasn't your usual sort of smuggler. For a start, he was a strict Methodist, and swearing was forbidden on any of his boats. He and his brothers Harry and Charles were, however, among the most successful smugglers in Cornwall during the late 1700s and early 1800s. Nicknamed 'the King of Prussia' in childhood games, Carter operated from three small coves to the east of Penzance – one of which was renamed Prussia Cove in his honour. The brothers sailed to France regularly, although on at least one occasion they clashed with the law. Despite this, their honesty was legendary. On one occasion, John Carter broke into the Custom House in Penzance to retrieve a delivery of tea that had been seized by excise officers. He was careful not to touch any of the contraband taken from other smugglers, however, and when the officers discovered the break-in they immediately knew that 'honest John' was responsible.

THE DEVIL WEARS BLACK (AND RED)

ONE OF THE CLASSIC INGREDIENTS of a Hollywood pirate is the Jolly Roger: a black flag bearing a white skull and crossbones. Yet, during the golden age of piracy, pirates hoisted a variety of individually designed 'house' flags atop their masts to strike fear into the hearts of their opponents. Most of these came in two colours: red, signifying that the attacker would give no mercy, and black, indicating death. Various motifs were used, but common themes were skeletons, bleeding hearts, hourglasses (symbols of death), cutlasses and, of course, skulls and crossbones. This design seems to have been originally flown by the Irish pirate Edward England, while the skull and crossed sabres depicted in the movie *The Pirates of the Caribbean* belonged to 'Calico Jack' Rackham. The name Jolly Roger may have originated in the original 'red duster' hoisted by fighting ships as a show of strength, and referred to ironically by the French as the Jolie Rouge ('pretty red').

 Yes, I do heartily repent; I repent I had not done more mischief, and that we did not cut the throats of them that took us, and I am extremely sorry that you ain't all hanged as well as we.

An anonymous pirate prior to being executed, quoted in
A General History of the Robberies and Murders of the Most Notorious Pyrates
by Captain Charles Johnson, published 1724

DID ANYONE REALLY WALK THE PLANK?

ACCORDING TO MYTHOLOGY, captives were made to walk the plank so their persecutors could avoid the charge of murder. The idea was that victims would be eaten by passing sharks or were weighted with stones so that they sank to the bottom and drowned. Either way, there are few reliable accounts of this practice taking place, and it seems unlikely in these circumstances that a defence of 'suicide' would stand up in a court of law. Walking the plank does, however, make great cinema.

3,250 MILES IN AN OPEN BOAT

Folk heroes come in all shapes and sizes, but Mary Bryant, one of Cornwall's most celebrated citizens, must be one of the most unusual. Convicted of assault and robbery in 1786, she was sentenced to seven years 'transportation' in Australia's penal colony. On the voyage out, she gave birth to a daughter Charlotte (named after the ship she was on) and met her future husband, Cornish fisherman William Bryant, whose child she gave birth to two years later. After three years in Australia, the couple, along with their two children and seven other convicts, made a daring escape when they sailed from Port Jackson to East Timor in an open boat, covering 3,250 miles (5,230km) in 69 days. It was a voyage every bit as challenging as Captain Bligh's, who had also fetched up in East Timor two years earlier. The Bryants and the other convicts were recaptured by the Dutch and sent back to Britain, although William and both children died of fever on the way. Back home, Mary was sentenced to an additional year's imprisonment but was eventually pardoned after a public outcry against the conviction.

Traditional pirate punch recipe

One of sour, two of sweet,
Three of strong and four of weak,
A dash of bitters and a sprinkle of spice,
Served well chilled with plenty of ice.

Or, to be exact:

One cup of lime juice, two cups of sugar syrup
Three cups of dark rum and four cups of tea
A dash of Angostura bitters and a sprinkle of nutmeg
Served well chilled with plenty of ice.

> I am sorry to see you here, but if you had fought
> like a man, you needn't be hang'd like a dog.

Anne Bonny to John 'Calico Jack' Rackham prior to his execution.
When the Royal Navy finally caught up with Rackham and his cohorts,
it is said only Bonny and Mary Read resisted arrest, the rest of the
crew being too drunk to fight.

WILL THE REAL DREAD PIRATE PLEASE STAND UP!

The above is an impossible request because, as anyone who has read William Goldman's novel *The Princess Bride* knows, there is no real Dread Pirate Roberts. Instead, the title is a *nom de guerre* secretly handed down from one individual to the next. So terrifying is the avatar's reputation – beyond anything a single individual could achieve – that whoever holds the title can loot and plunder at will. Once he has done enough pirating, the title-holder chooses a successor. The rest of the crew is then dismissed, the old Roberts hands over to his successor, and a new crew is brought on board. The old Roberts stays on as First Mate just long enough to ensure the new crew believe the scam, and then slips off to enjoy his ill-gotten gains. At the point we join the pirate action in Goldman's novel, there have been four incarnations of the Dread Pirate: the original Roberts, who retired 15 years previously; Clooney, the original Roberts' first mate; Cummerbund; and Ryan. The book's hero Westley becomes the fifth Dread Pirate, although who succeeds him isn't exactly clear.

PIRATES IN SHAKESPEARE

'The Shakespearean pirate [...] should be understood finally as a metaphor for the intrusion of a just Providence in the affairs of men, indeed a symbol of God's active government of the world stage.'
'Shakespeare and the Pirates' by Richard S Ide, in *Iowa State Journal of Research*, 58, 1984

THE REAL ROBINSON CRUSOE

Proof that real life is stranger than fiction is the unlikely story of the Scottish ne'er-do-well Alexander Selkirk. At the age of 19, he ran off to sea to make his fortune on a privateer – which was effectively a pirate ship that was paid by the King to attack his enemies. In 1704, after a particularly damaging encounter with the Spaniards on board the 16-gun galleon *Cinque Ports*, he decided the ship was unsafe and demanded to be put ashore on the next island. He was accordingly dropped off on Más a Tierra, a deserted island 400 miles of the coast of Peru, with some bedding, a musket, a few tools and a Bible. For the next four years, he learned to live by his wits, foraging for food, hunting goats, building huts out of pimento trees and making clothes from goat skins. He was eventually rescued by another privateer and given his own command, from which position he continued to attack Spanish treasure ships until his return to England two years later. His story was widely reported and quickly turned into a bestselling book by Daniel Defoe, who immortalised Selkirk as Robinson Crusoe. His decision to abandon ship was completely vindicated when the *Cinque Ports* was shipwrecked and all its crew killed, apart from the captain and seven men, who were captured and thrown in a Peruvian jail.

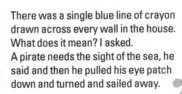

There was a single blue line of crayon drawn across every wall in the house. What does it mean? I asked.
A pirate needs the sight of the sea, he said and then he pulled his eye patch down and turned and sailed away.

Story People: Selected Stories and Drawings by Brian Andreas, 1997

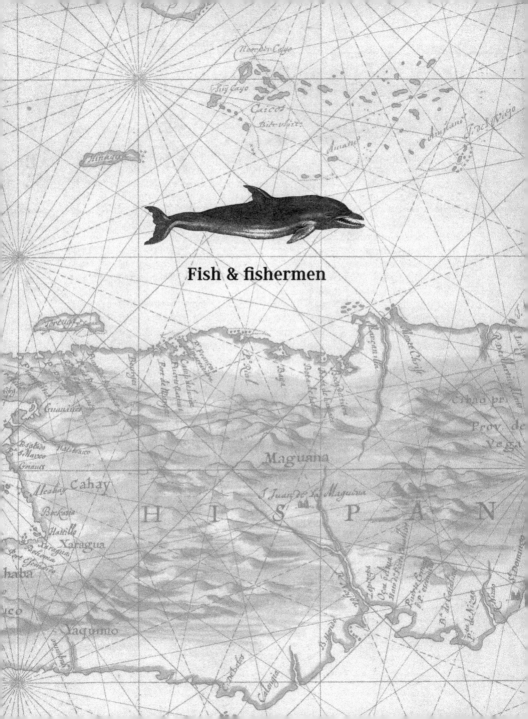

Fish & fishermen

UNITED NATIONS CONVENTION ON THE LAW OF THE SEA, 1982

Article 119: Conservation of the living resources of the high seas
'1. In determining the allowable catch and establishing other conservation measures for the living resources in the high seas, States shall:
   (a) take measures which are designed, on the best scientific evidence available to the States concerned, to maintain or restore populations of harvested species at levels which can produce the maximum sustainable yield, as qualified by relevant environmental and economic factors, including the special requirements of developing States, and taking into account fishing patterns, the interdependence of stocks and any generally recommended international minimum standards, whether subregional, regional or global;
   (b) take into consideration the effects on species associated with or dependent upon harvested species with a view to maintaining or restoring populations of such associated or dependent species above levels at which their reproduction may become seriously threatened.
2. Available scientific information, catch and fishing effort statistics, and other data relevant to the conservation of fish stocks shall be contributed and exchanged on a regular basis through competent international organizations, whether subregional, regional or global, where appropriate and with participation by all States concerned.
3. States concerned shall ensure that conservation measures and their implementation do not discriminate in form or in fact against the fishermen of any State.'

Top ten catchers of fish		Top ten eaters of fish	
China	9.9 million tonnes	China	13.6 million tonnes
Peru	8.3 million tonnes	Japan	9 million tonnes
USA	4.9 million tonnes	USA	4.7 million tonnes
Japan	4.4 million tonnes	Indonesia	3.6 million tonnes
Chile	4.2 million tonnes	India	3.1 million tonnes
Indonesia	4.2 million tonnes	South Korea	2.7 million tonnes
India	3.4 million tonnes	Thailand	2.4 million tonnes
Russia	3.1 million tonnes	Russia	2.1 million tonnes
Thailand	2.6 million tonnes	Philippines	2.1 million tonnes
Norway	2.6 million tonnes	Nigeria	1.8 million tonnes

Figures in metric tonnes   *Figures in metric tonnes*

Source: University of British Columbia Fisheries Centre

SEAHORSES: LOVE FOR LIFE?

THE IDEA THAT SEAHORSES ARE MONOGAMOUS and mate for life appeals to the romantic in all of us. Trouble is, it's almost certainly not true. The story originates from a study of one specific species of seahorse, *Hippocampus whitei*, over one reproductive cycle. Studies of other species of seahorse suggest that they are far from monogamous, with some, such as *Hippocampus breviceps*, breeding in groups and pairing up with any partner available. Size seems to be the main attraction, and if a male seahorse meets a bigger female seahorse in between broods, he will readily swap partners. Even *Hippocampus whitei* is now thought to change partner between families. That said, once they are paired off, seahorses do engage in a long romantic ritual lasting several days and culminating in a courtship dance that includes holding tails and snout-to-snout 'kissing'. The female then deposits hundreds of eggs into the male's pouch, which he carries for several weeks before giving birth to fully formed baby seahorses. Only about five in 1,000 will survive to adulthood. Within hours of giving birth, the male seahorse is ready to mate again.

BIG AS A CAR

Despite better fishing technology and the proliferation of big-game fishing as a sport, the record for the biggest marlin ever caught still dates back to 1953. That was when Alfred C Glassnell Jnr caught his 1,560lb (708kg) giant off Cabo Blanco in Peru. Just to put that in perspective, 1,500lb is the weight of a large polar bear, or a small car such as a Triumph Spitfire or a Lotus Elise.

THE DEADLIEST TRADE

Commercial fishing is one of the most dangerous occupations in the USA, recording an average of 58 deaths per year from 1992 to 2008. That's 128 per 100,000 fishermen – 32 times more than the national average of 4 per 100,000 for all workers. Most deaths were the result of vessel accidents (52 per cent), followed by falling overboard (31 per cent) and accidents aboard ship (10 per cent). The most common vessel accident was flooding (28 per cent), followed by instability (18 per cent), large waves (18 per cent) and collision (10 per cent). The most dangerous region was Alaska (25 per cent), followed by the North-east (25 per cent), the Gulf of Mexico (23 per cent) and the West Coast (16 per cent). The most dangerous type of fishing was shellfish (47 per cent), followed by groundfish (30 per cent) and pelagic (that is, surface) fish (20 per cent).

THE YEAR NO ONE DIED

The year 2008 was a special one for Iceland. It was the first year since records began that no deaths at sea were recorded. Quite possibly, that means it was the first year since the country was settled more than 1,000 years ago that no one died at sea. An estimated 4,000 people have been killed at sea in Iceland in the last century alone – an average of 40 people a year, or more than three a month. Improved safety and better shipbuilding were both credited with contributing to the improved figures, plus the fact that there are fewer fishermen than there were before.

IS NEMO A GIRL?

The movie *Finding Nemo* shot the colourful clownfish into popular consciousness – so much so that sales of the species trebled after the film was released in 2003. Less well known are the unusual gender politics of the species. In essence, all clownfish are born male but aspire to become female. Once they become female, however, there's no going back. It goes something like this. Clownfish live in harems based around a host anemone. Each harem has one large, ruling female that mates with the dominant male, while a clutch of juvenile males waits in the wings. If the ruling female dies, the dominant male turns into a female, simultaneously increasing in size. The biggest juvenile then takes over as the dominant male and mates with the previous dominant male, now turned ruling female. Although strictly speaking, Nemo is a 'false' clownfish (*Amphiprion ocellaris*), which is subtly different from a 'true' clownfish (*Amphiprion percula*), it is also a hermaphrodite species – which means one day he might be a she.

EVERY SCALE TELLS A STORY

EVERYONE KNOWS you can tell the age of a tree by counting the number of growth rings in its trunk, but how can you tell the age of fish? Strangely enough, the same way. Fish go through seasonal growth patterns, usually growing more during the summer months than in winter. As their scales grow in proportion with the rest of their bodies, these seasonal patterns are visible as growth rings on their scales. During periods of fast growth, the rings are widely spaced, while during periods of slow growth they become darker and more closely spaced. Each set of rings therefore represents a year of the fish's life. This phenomenon was first discovered by the Dutch scientist Antony van Leeuwenhoek in 1684 but was not widely accepted until it was rediscovered in the late 1800s.

A brief history of cod

800s   Vikings head south and start trading dried cod with other European countries.

1300s   Hanseatic League controls valuable dried-cod trade in northern Europe.

1400s   Portuguese fishermen discover cod fisheries off Newfoundland, probably preceding John Cabot's 'discovery' of America.

1700s   Cod-fishing fleets are established in Gloucester, Salem, Dorchester and Marblehead in Massachusetts, leading to the creation of the 'cod aristocracy'.

1763   British Prime Minister William Pitt the Elder criticises the decision to give Newfoundland fishing rights to France and describes cod as 'British gold'.

1951   Improvements in technology such as sonar mean fishing boats can fish deeper, further and longer than ever before, leading to so-called 'factory fishing'.

1968   Newfoundland cod catch peaks at 810,000 tons (735,000 tonnes).

1970s   The so-called 'cod wars' between Iceland and UK over fishing rights in the North Atlantic lead to rammings and sabotage. The UK eventually drops its claims.

1983   The EU introduces species-by-species fish quotas, including one for cod.

1992   Canada bans cod fishing on the Grand Banks.

2000   The World Wildlife Fund places cod on its Endangered Species list.

MAN OF IRON

Fishing is a notoriously tough life and fishermen are a notoriously tough lot, but few are tougher than the legendary Howard Blackburn. The Massachusetts doryman was fishing on the Grand Banks in January 1883 when he and his fishing mate lost sight of their base ship, the schooner *Grace L Fears*, in a blizzard. It took him five days to row his 19ft (5.8m) open boat to shore. Having lost his heavy fishing mittens over the side, he kept going by deliberately freezing his hands into hooks to keep hold of the oars. 'It is surprising how fast dead flesh disintegrates when rubbed hard,' he said. 'In a short space of time it seemed as though I was holding the oars with bones and muscles only.' By the time he reached land, he had lost all his fingers and both thumbs to the first joint as well as one toe. His fishing mate died on the way. He became a hero in his home town of Gloucester, Massachusetts and opened a successful saloon. He later sailed across the Atlantic twice on his own, setting a new record of 39 days in 1901. He almost died on his third attempt, this time in a small dory like the one he used to fish from. Some people just never seem to learn…

HEMINGWAY'S MILE

ERNEST HEMINGWAY loved fishing, and he loved Cuba, where he lived on and off for more than 20 years. So what better way to honour him than to create a fishing competition off Havana in his name? The first Hemingway International Billfishing Tournament was launched in May 1950, and has been held every year since, except for in 1961 and 1962 when tension between Cuba and the USA was at its peak. As you'd expect of an event named after the author of *The Old Man and the Sea*, the competition is for big game fishing, such as marlin and tuna – although nowadays the fish are released back into the sea, something the notoriously uncompromising Hemingway would surely have scoffed at. The author not only agreed to lend his name to the event, but won the first three tournaments on his boat *Pilar*. Cuba's president, Fidel Castro, won it in 1960.

COMMANDO DOLPHINS

Dolphins have long been regarded as a sailor's best friend, and stories abound of crew rescued by dolphins and ships led to safety. The US Navy took this collaboration to new levels during the Iraq war when it trained a school of bottlenose dolphins to locate anti-shipping mines in the Persian Gulf. The animals' sonar abilities are so acute that they can detect the mines even when they are buried in a seabed cluttered with other debris – something no artificial device can do. Once the mines are located, the dolphins drop a transponder nearby, so their human colleagues can locate and destroy the device. And all in return for a few scraps of fish. The navy also uses sea lions to retrieve objects from the sea floor, attach devices and locate enemy divers. A symbiotic relationship or animal exploitation?

'Red herring'

The origins of this expression is usually traced to the practice of using herring to cover a scent while training hunting dogs – the idea being to teach the dogs not to be thrown off the real scent. This explanation is, however, itself a bit of a red herring. It's more likely the training technique was used as a metaphor by author William Cobbett in his *Political Register* in 1807 and has since been taken much too literally. The herring is described as red because it has been smoked and turned into kipper, and is therefore especially pungent.

HOW A SHIPWORM BUILT THE CHANNEL TUNNEL

We can thank the destructive behaviour of a tiny shipworm for the construction of the Channel Tunnel. It was while observing *Teredo navalis* – a worm-like creature that burrows its way through wooden ships – that Marc Brunel (father of Isambard) came up with an innovative method for digging a tunnel through soft ground. Brunel noticed that, as the teredo ate away the wood, it excreted a substance that lined the tunnel behind it.

He imitated this technique by creating a tunnelling shield with removable sections that were gradually moved forward as the tunnel was mined at the front, and filled in and lined with bricks from behind. The method was first used in 1805 on the Thames Tunnel at Rotherhithe, UK and was also used for the construction of the Channel Tunnel – except four 27ft (8.2m)-diameter boring machines replaced miners with pickaxes.

QUEL MONSTROUS MOLLUSC!

'I LOOKED IN MY TURN, and could not repress a gesture of disgust. Before my eyes was a horrible monster worthy to figure in the legends of the marvellous. It was an immense cuttlefish, being eight yards long. It swam crossways in the direction of the *Nautilus* with great speed, watching us with its enormous staring green eyes. Its eight arms, or rather feet, fixed to its head, that have given the name of cephalopod to these animals, were twice as long as its body, and were twisted like the furies' hair. One could see the 250 air holes on the inner side of the tentacles. The monster's mouth, a horned beak like a parrot's, opened and shut vertically. Its tongue, a horned substance, furnished with several rows of pointed teeth, came out quivering from this veritable pair of shears. What a freak of nature, a bird's beak on a mollusc! Its spindle-like body formed a fleshy mass that might weigh 4,000 to 5,000lb; the varying colour changing with great rapidity, according to the irritation of the animal, passed successively from livid grey to reddish brown. What irritated this mollusc? No doubt the presence of the *Nautilus*, more formidable than itself, and on which its suckers or its jaws had no hold. Yet, what monsters these poulps are! What vitality the Creator has given them! What vigour in their movements! And they possess three hearts! Chance had brought us in presence of this cuttlefish, and I did not wish to lose the opportunity of carefully studying this specimen of cephalopods. I overcame the horror that inspired me, and, taking a pencil, began to draw it.'

Source: *Twenty Thousand Leagues Under the Sea*
by Jules Verne, 1869

Ten most endangered fish

According to the 'red list' published by the International Union for Conservation of Nature, 1,414 species of fish, or 5 per cent of all species, are at risk of extinction. This is mostly due to over-fishing or destruction of habitat. With so many species on the list and so little known about most of them, any top ten is likely to be subjective. Here are some of the better-known contenders.

Bluefin tuna – With each fish fetching up to $100,000, stocks of bluefin tuna have plummeted by 85 per cent in 36 years, making it a very endangered species indeed.

Blue whale – The biggest creature in the world (ever) used to number up to 220,000, but most estimates now put them at fewer than 5,000.

Hector's dolphin – The smallest dolphin, at just 4ft (1.2m) long, this species is now also the rarest, with only 7,000 left. They are usually killed as a by-catch of trawling.

Atlantic halibut – Halibut can grow up to 9ft (2.7m) long and live up to 50 years. The USA has banned halibut fishing in coastal waters, but they are often killed as by-catch.

Goliath grouper – A large fish with a short reproductive cycle, the Goliath grouper can live for up to 40 years. Harvesting is banned in the USA.

European eel – Although born at sea, European eels spend most of their lives in fresh water before returning to sea to spawn. They are usually caught mid-journey.

Beluga sturgeon – A native of the Caspian Sea, the beluga produces the most expensive caviar in the world. Over-fishing means it is now under threat.

Maltese ray – Once prolific throughout the Mediterranean, this ray is now mainly found in the Strait of Sicily. It's often killed as a by-catch and thrown back in the sea.

Angel shark – More like an oversized ray than a shark, the angel shark is thought to be extinct in the Atlantic and Mediterranean, and under serious threat elsewhere.

Winter skate – A native of the US North Atlantic coast, the population of mature winter skate is said to have declined by 90 per cent since the 1970s.

GREENPEACE'S RED LIST

GREENPEACE INTERNATIONAL has produced its own 'red list' of fish 'that are commonly sold in supermarkets around the world, and which have a very high risk of being sourced from unsustainable fisheries'. It includes: anglerfish, tuna, Atlantic cod, shark, eel, haddock, hake, Atlantic halibut, Greenland halibut, hoki, marlin, European plaice, red fish, orange roughy, Atlantic salmon, tropical shrimp, skates and rays, sole, swordfish and toothfish. See www.greenpeace.org.

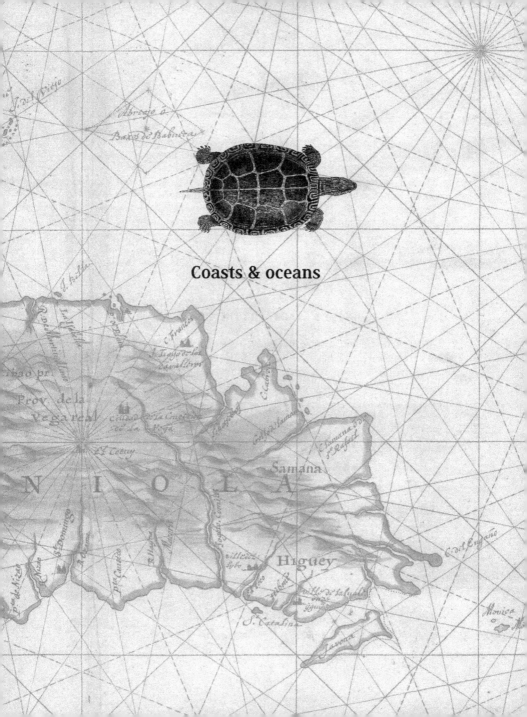

Coasts & oceans

HOW SALTY IS THE SEA?

The average salt content of seawater is 3.5 per cent. Its salinity, however, varies from place to place, particularly in isolated bodies of water. The Dead Sea has the highest salt content, with an astonishing 33 per cent in certain parts, while the Baltic Sea has the lowest, with an average of just 0.5 per cent. The higher the salt content, the greater the buoyancy of the water, which is why it's so easy to float in the Dead Sea – and why Scandinavians are such good swimmers (joke!). According to the National Oceanic and Atmospheric Administration, if all the salt in the sea was taken out and sprinkled over the land, it would form a layer more than 500ft (150m) deep, or about the height of a 40-floor building. You can soon see the difference between salt and fresh water by leaving a container of each to evaporate in the sunlight. Whereas 1ft³ (0.03m³) of seawater will yield about 2.2lb (1kg) of salt, the same amount of fresh water will yield just 0.03oz (1 gram).

LET'S HEAR IT FOR THE OCEANS

About 71 per cent of the Earth's surface is covered in water, of which 97.5 per cent is sea. That's 140 million square miles (362 million km²) of ocean – or 37 times the size of the USA. Its average temperature is 2 degrees C (39 degrees F), it contains 95 per cent of the Earth's liveable space and produces 75 per cent of the world's oxygen.

LET'S HEAR IT FOR THE COASTS

According to the United Nations, 60 per cent of the world's population – that's 3.6 billion people – live within 37 miles (60km) of the coast, and that figure is likely to rise to 75 per cent in the next 20 years. Coastal areas also provide habitat for 90 per cent of marine species, including 80 per cent of the world's fish. Coastal areas also host 80 per cent of all tourism, leading some to speculate that tourists are like fish.

JURASSIC CARP

The biggest fish from the Jurassic era was the 88-ft (27-m) Leedsichthys. Despite its enormous size, this ungainly giant survived on a diet of plankton – just like the current biggest fish, the blue whale. The Leedsichthys had 40,000 teeth in the back of its mouth that acted as a sieve to extract plankton from the water. It had no means of defence, apart from its enormous size, and it was not uncommon for other, more uncouth, fish to help themselves to chunks of its body for their dinner. This made the Leedsichthys sad and may have contributed to its extinction.

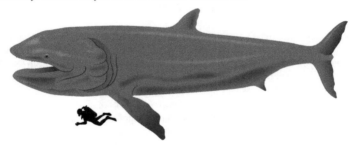

FREEDOM OF THE HIGH SEAS

MANY PEOPLE DREAM of setting off on adventures on the high seas, but how many realise the term has a specific legal meaning? According to international law, 'high seas' refers to the mass of sea that is beyond any country's jurisdiction – that is, the area outside the 12-mile (19-km) belt of territorial waters that extends from a country's coast. There have been many attempts to agree a set of laws for the high seas, including several United Nation conferences, but the laws are notoriously difficult to enforce. The 1982 Convention on the Law of the Sea asserts the following freedoms: the right to peaceful navigation, fishing, laying underwater cables and pipelines, and flying overhead. It also stipulates measures for the conservation of its sea life and the ecosystem. Beyond that, the behaviour of ships is governed by the country whose flag they fly, which can lead to conflict – particularly in the Arctic and Antarctic, areas of which several countries claim ownership.

WHY YOU SHOULDN'T ASK SANTA FOR A CORAL NECKLACE

CORAL MIGHT LOOK LIKE SO MUCH CRUNCHY MACARONI, but those magical multicoloured shapes are actually the home of a tiny polyp. Closely related to the sea anemone and the jellyfish, the polyp has tiny, tentacular arms that it uses to reach out and grab passing food, mostly small animals. It becomes coral when it fastens itself to a rock and creates an outer skeleton out of limestone. As it divides and reproduces itself, new polyps attach themselves to the old and build up over years to create reefs. Some corals reefs are thought to be more than 50 million years old. Although coral reefs only cover 1 per cent of the seabed, the ecosystems they provide are so productive they support 25 per cent of all sea creatures. These reefs are under threat from pollution, fishing, tourism and climate change, with as much as 60 per cent of the remaining reefs in immediate danger. One sign of this is increased 'bleaching'. Corals gain their colours by hosting algae, which they reject when under stress. The number of incidents of coral bleaching has gone up dramatically in recent years, suggesting corals are increasingly stressed.

KILLER PLASTIC

They're called mermaid's tears and can be found on every beach from the Costa Brava to Hawaii. Every year, millions of tiny bits of plastic, officially called nurdles, find their way into the ocean. They come from plastic blown into the sea, from litter left on the beach and rubbish thrown over the side of ships. Every year these mermaid's tears and other plastic debris kills up to one million seabirds, 100,000 sea mammals, and countless fish. Nurdles and much larger bits of plastic – such as combs, toothbrushes, syringes and tampon applicators – are all commonly found in the stomachs of seabirds and turtles. In one area of the Pacific, plastic has accumulated in a great pea soup called the Great Pacific Garbage Patch, which is thought to be twice the size of France. No wonder the mermaids are crying.

> The lure of the sea is some strange magic that makes men love what they fear. The solitude of the desert is more intimate than that of the sea. Death on the shifting barren sands seems less insupportable to the imagination than death out on the boundless ocean, in the awful, windy emptiness.
>
> Zane Grey, US author (1872–1939)

WHERE TWO OCEANS MEET

What happens when rivers meet the sea? The usual effect is a kind of blurring where the two waters meet – not unlike a heat haze. The phenomenon is called halocline and can be seen anywhere a stream pours into the sea. Where great bodies of water are concerned, the effect is more dramatic. Photos taken by a passenger on a cruise ship in the Gulf of Alaska show a line of froth several miles long, with turquoise water on one side and darker water on the other. The images appear to show the fresh water from a melting polar glacier meeting the saltier water of the Pacific Ocean. Rather than mixing immediately, as you'd expect, the two waters have created a distinct boundary. Nature, it turns out, is not always as seamless as we might imagine. One of the images, incidentally, went viral and attracted over 177,000 views in one day.

THE SEA WITH NO SHORES

ON 20 SEPTEMBER 1492, halfway across the Atlantic, Christopher Columbus came across a vast patch of seaweed 'stretching to the north as far as you can see'. The seaweed contained a whole ecosystem, with many of the small fish, crabs and shrimps found close to shore, leading the crew of the *Santa Maria* to conclude they must be nearing land. In fact, they had stumbled on the Sargasso Sea. Caught between the currents that sweep around the edges of the Atlantic, this mass of seaweed is suspended in mid-ocean, providing a sanctuary for creatures such as loggerhead turtles and young tuna. Some species of eel are thought to lay their eggs there, before returning to the coasts of Europe and North America. Historically, the area was feared as it was thought the seaweed slowed ships down or even swallowed them up. A large body of literature has built up around this idea, including poems by Ezra Pound and Dylan Thomas. Increasingly, the Sargasso Sea is also attracting a large concentration of rubbish, particularly plastic.

> It is an interesting biological fact that all of us have, in our veins the exact same percentage of salt in our blood that exists in the ocean, and, therefore, we have salt in our blood, in our sweat, in our tears. We are tied to the ocean. And when we go back to the sea, whether it is to sail or to watch it, we are going back from whence we came.
>
> John F Kennedy, US president (1917–63)

Countries with the longest coastlines

Canada	125,567 miles (202,080km)	Japan	18,486 miles (29,751km)
Indonesia	33,998 miles (54,716km)	Australia	16,006 miles (25,760km)
Greenland (Denmark)	27,394 miles (44,087km)	Norway	15,626 miles (25,148km)
		United States	12,380 miles (19,924km)
Russia	23,397 miles (37,653km)	New Zealand	9,404 miles (15,134km)
The Philippines	22,549 miles (36,289km)		

Source: *CIA World Factbook*

THAT DROWNING FEELING

A PENDING GLOBAL CATASTROPHE or 'the greatest lie ever told'? Global warming and the associated rise in sea levels is one of the most controversial issues of our age. According to figures released by the Intergovernmental Panel on Climate Change (IPCC), by 2100 sea levels will rise by at least 7in (18cm) and possibly up to 23in (59cm). This would mean that islands such as Tuvalu and the Maldives would be virtually wiped out. The reason given for this is the increase in temperature caused by fossil-fuel emissions trapped in Earth's atmosphere. This causes the sea to warm up and expand, forcing sea levels up. There is also widespread evidence of the polar ice caps melting, adding to the volume of water. Not everyone agrees with this, however, and no less a figure than the former chairman of the International Union for Quaternary Science (INQUA) and International Commission on Sea Level Change, Nils-Axel Mörner, insists sea levels haven't risen in the past 50 years. Who to believe? It's not terribly scientific, but surely a time-proven proverb applies here: 'Better safe than sorry'.

POWER TO THE POLYP

The largest living creature on Earth or the largest structure made by a living creature? However you think of the Barrier Reef (it's made from the skeletons of millions of tiny creatures called polyps), there's no doubt it's big. At 1,250 miles (2,012km) long and up to 40 miles (65km) wide, it's the only living creature (or the only structure made by a living creature*) visible from outer space. In 1997, it was named by broadcaster CNN one of the Seven Natural Wonders of the World.

* According to NASA, it's an urban myth that the Great Wall of China is visible from outer space.

BIG ICE

THE TALLEST ICEBERG ever seen was a 550ft (168m)-high specimen spotted off the coast of Greenland by the American icebreaker *East Wind* in 1958. Bearing in mind that only about 10 per cent of an iceberg is visible above water, this suggests that *East Wind*'s iceberg was nearly 5,000ft (1,525m) deep. Another iceberg spotted in the Southern Ocean by the USS *Glacier* in 1956 was estimated to have an area of over 12,000 square miles (31,000km²) – bigger than the whole of Belgium.

THE ORIGINS OF SCUBA

Assisted diving started in the 4th century BC, when the Greek philosopher Aristotle recorded the first known use of a diving bell: an upside-down cauldron that was dragged underwater to provide a supply of air. Things got a little more sophisticated in the 16th century, when purpose-made diving bells – including one designed by Leonardo da Vinci – were widely used. The invention of the air pump in 1771 allowed a constant supply of air to be pumped into the bell and brought the dream of underwater exploration a step nearer. The next step was to design a diving suit, to give divers more autonomy. There had been attempts to design one since at least 1405, but the classic diving suit was invented in 1837 by the German/British engineer Augustus Siebbe. Even Houdini, the escapologist, took an interest and invented a suit from which the diver could quickly escape in an emergency. But the era of modern scuba diving was born in 1943 when Emile Gagnan and Jacques Cousteau launched their Aqua-Lung air regulator, which – combined with compressed air tanks – allowed divers to roam freely underwater for the first time. And the origins of the word scuba? Well it's an acronym – SCUBA: self-contained underwater breathing apparatus, of course!

'Between the devil and the deep blue sea'

A popular explanation for the origins of this expression is that the outer plank of a ship's deck was called the 'devil'. If the seam between the devil and the top of the hull needed caulking while at sea, a sailor would have to be suspended over the side of the vessel in a bosun's chair, putting him in a precarious position between the devil and the deep blue sea. It's a lovely idea only slightly undermined by the fact that the first recorded use of the expression predates that of the nautical term by about 200 years.

DEEPER THAN EVEREST

MOST OF THE WORLD IS SEA. Nearly 71 per cent of the planet's surface is covered by sea – and not just a bit of sea, but loads of it. More than half the sea is more than 9,800ft (3,000m) deep. Its deepest point is the Mariana Trench in the Pacific Ocean, near Japan, which is estimated to be over 36,000ft (11,000m) deep – that's 7,200ft (2,200m) deeper than Mount Everest is tall. Most of the seabed is unexplored and scientists have, frankly, no idea what's down there. We know much more about the surface of the Moon than we know about the bottom of the sea. Get diving!

Biggest, coldest, saltiest

- The largest sea is the Bering Sea at 876,000 square miles (2,270,000km²).
- Deepest point: 36,198ft (11,033m) in the Mariana Trench, western Pacific.
- The warmest sea in the world is the Red Sea, where temperatures range from 20°C (68°F) to 31°C (87.8°F), depending upon which part you measure.
- The coldest seas are, not surprisingly, found near the poles – such as the Greenland, Barents, Beaufort, Kara, Laptev and East Siberian seas near the north pole, and the Weddell and Ross seas near the south pole.
- Depending upon the amount of salt in the water, seawater freezes at about minus 2 degrees C (28 degrees F) – 4 degrees F colder than fresh water. High salt content lowers the temperature for freezing and low salt content raises the temperature for freezing.

THE BIG BLUE

It's a common misconception that the sea is blue because it reflects the sky. This idea is based on the observation that a small amount of seawater placed in a glass looks clear, therefore the colour must come from elsewhere. But the sea is in fact intrinsically blue – it's just that it's a very pale shade of blue. The deeper the sea, the darker the colour. In shallow waters, the colour of the seabed also plays a crucial part. A sandy bottom will produce turquoise, while seaweed can make the sea look almost black. The only time the colour of the sky really has an impact is when the sea is flat and calm – then the surface acts like a giant mirror.

HOW MANY SEAS?

In classical times, the Seven Seas referred to the Mediterranean Sea, the Adriatic Sea, the Indian Ocean, the Black Sea, the Caspian Sea, the Persian Gulf and the Red Sea. Arabian writers also referred to the Seven Seas, but they had a completely different set of seas in mind, mostly located in the Middle East and Asia. Given half a chance, the Ancient Greeks also liked to throw in the Aegean Sea. In modern times, the idea of Four Oceans gained more credence, namely the Atlantic Ocean, the Pacific Ocean, the Indian Ocean, and the Arctic Sea – until 2000, when the International Hydrographic Organisation officially recognised the Southern Ocean, the ring of sea around Antarctica up to 60 degrees South, bringing the tally up to five. Any more, anyone?

Ocean's Five

Pacific Ocean	60,060,000 square miles (155,557,000km²)
Atlantic Ocean	29,637,000 square miles (76,762,000km²)
Indian Ocean	26,469,000 square miles (68,556,000km²)
Southern Ocean*	7,848,000 square miles (20,327,000km²)
Arctic Sea	5,427,000 square miles (14,056,000km²)

*New entry

GIANTS OF THE SEA

A FERTILE SEABED, WARM WATER AND SUNLIGHT combine to turn the sea into a fantastic habitat for wildlife. Coastal waters, in particular, are rich in biodiversity. Scientists have already catalogued 120,000 species in the sea, and they estimate there are at least 750,000 more to be discovered. The largest of these is the blue whale, which weighs in at up to 186 tons (190 tonnes) and more than 100ft (30m) long – that's nearly 18 times the weight of the largest elephant, and 25 times the weight of a double-decker bus. It's thought to be the largest animal ever to have existed on Earth (much bigger than Tyrannosaurus rex). It's also one of the most endangered species on Earth, with less than 15,000 left alive.

UNITED NATIONS CONVENTION ON THE LAW OF THE SEA, 1982

Article 88: Reservation of the high seas for peaceful purposes
'The high seas shall be reserved for peaceful purposes.
Article 89: Invalidity of claims of sovereignty over the high seas
No State may validly purport to subject any part of the high seas to its sovereignty.
Article 90: Right of navigation
Every State, whether coastal or land-locked, has the right to sail ships flying its flag on the high seas.'

THE ORIGIN OF MANY SPECIES

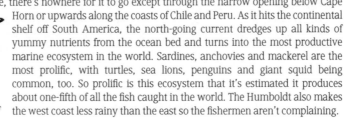

Ever wondered why the west coast of South America is so much colder than the east coast? It's all because of the Humboldt Current. Named after the Prussian naturalist Alexander von Humboldt, the current is driven by the prevailing westerly winds of the Southern Ocean, which drive the sea towards the southern tip of the continent. Once it gets there, there's nowhere for it to go except through the narrow opening below Cape Horn or upwards along the coasts of Chile and Peru. As it hits the continental shelf off South America, the north-going current dredges up all kinds of yummy nutrients from the ocean bed and turns into the most productive marine ecosystem in the world. Sardines, anchovies and mackerel are the most prolific, with turtles, sea lions, penguins and giant squid being common, too. So prolific is this ecosystem that it's estimated it produces about one-fifth of all the fish caught in the world. The Humboldt also makes the west coast less rainy than the east so the fishermen aren't complaining.

> ❝ He always thought of the sea as "la mar" which is what people call her in Spanish when they love her. Sometimes those who love her say bad things of her but they are always said as though she were a woman. Some of the younger fishermen, those who used buoys as floats for their lines and had motorboats, bought when the shark livers had brought much money, spoke of her as "el mar" which is masculine. They spoke of her as a contestant or a place or even an enemy. But the old man always thought of her as feminine and as something that gave or withheld great favours, and if she did wild or wicked things it was because she could not help them. The moon affects her as it does a woman, he thought. ❞
>
> *The Old Man and the Sea* by Ernest Hemingway, 1952

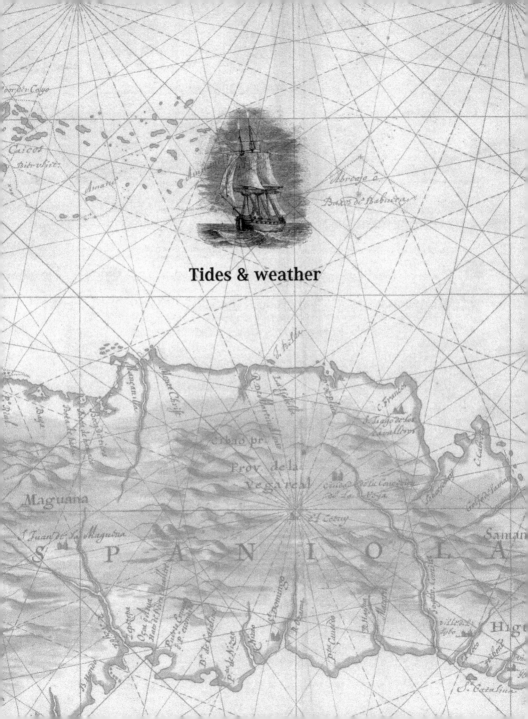

Tides & weather

WEATHER LORE 1

'Red sky at night, shepherd's delight,
Red sky in morning, sailor's warning.'

As the weather systems in the northern hemisphere travel from west to east, the early morning Sun rising in the east will light up moisture-bearing clouds arriving from the west. Conversely, the evening Sun setting in the west will light up departing clouds in the east. More generally, a clear sky in the west in the evening is associated with a high pressure system and prolonged clear weather. So accurate is this prediction, that it's been replicated in several other languages.

IN FRENCH:
'Rouge le soir, bel espoir,
Rouge le matin, de la pluie en chemin.'
(*'Red at night, good hope, Red in the morning, rain is on its way.'*)

IN NORWEGIAN:
'Morgenrode gir dage blode,
Kveldsrode gir dage sode.'
(*'Morning red gives wet days, Evening red gives sweet days.'*)

IN ITALIAN:
'Rosso di sera, bel tempo si spera,
rosso di mattina, mal tempo si avvicina.'
(*'Red sky at night, good weather is hoped for,
Red in the morning, bad weather is approaching.'*)

WHERE DOES THE GULF STREAM BEGIN?

THIS IS A CHICKEN AND EGG QUESTION, and the answer is determined as much by national prejudice as scientific fact. The Gulf Stream is caused by two factors. The surface water of the North Atlantic is cooled by Arctic winds and sinks to the bottom of the ocean, before heading south to the Equator. There, it is warmed and driven westwards by the prevailing westerly winds. So it's the combination of Arctic cooling and African winds that drive the water. But the current only resurfaces when it reaches the Gulf of Mexico and heads northwards again, which is why it's said to 'start' in the Gulf of Mexico (or off Florida) and is known as the Gulf Stream. In any case, its effect on the climate of the east coast of America and northern Europe is enormous. Without the Gulf Stream and its associated North Atlantic Drift, it's estimated temperatures in London would be at least 5 degrees C lower, or an average of 5 degrees C (40 degrees F) year-round – on a par with Newfoundland, which is on the same latitude. The Gulf Stream's far-reaching influence also allows ports in the Baltic, which would otherwise become ice bound, to remain open all year round.

YOU SPIN ME ROUND, CORIOLIS

One of the more interesting ideas promoted by popular science is that water draining out of a sink in the northern hemisphere spins in the opposite direction than in the southern hemisphere. The phenomenon referred to is the Coriolis effect, by which objects not connected to the ground (e.g. missiles) are pulled to the east due to the rotation of the earth. Since points near the Equator travel faster around the Earth's axis than points near the poles, objects which start their trajectory near the equator will have a greater pull eastwards than objects which start nearer the poles. That means that if the object travels far enough north or south, then its eastward pull will be different from the ground beneath. The phenomenon, discovered by the French engineer Gustave-Gaspard Coriolis in 1835, affects the movement of air over the Earth's surface and has enormous implications for our weather patterns. Thanks to the Coriolis effect, the trade winds tend to come from the east or the west, rather than straight from the north or south. It also dictates the direction of high- and low-pressure systems. However, the Coriolis effect only works on large masses travelling a long way, so while it may have a faint action on water in a sink, its effect will be so small as to be nil. That idea is bunkum.

Largest tidal range

Minas Basin, Bay of Fundy, Nova Scotia, Canada	53.5ft (16.3m)
Leaf Basin, Ungava Bay, Quebec, Canada	53.1ft (16.2m)
Burnham-in-Sea, Bristol Channel, UK	49ft (15m)
Derby, King Sound, Western Australia	approx 40ft (12m)
Gulf of Khambhat, Gujarat, India	approx 40ft (12m)
Cook Inlet, Alaska	approx 40ft (12m)

MINI-TIDES

THE SMALLEST TIDES – as little as 1in (2.5cm) – occur in the Mediterranean Sea, the Baltic Sea and the Caribbean Sea. Almost zero tidal areas (which are called amphidromic points) occur within the Mediterranean just south of Sicily, two-thirds of the way up the Adriatic Sea, in most of the Aegean Sea, in the Libyan Sea, and they can also be found in a large area around Ibiza.

THE BATTLE OF THE WASH

Y OU MIGHT NOT THINK having the highest tides in the world would necessarily be anything to boast about. After all, high tides flood cellars, sink cars and play havoc with boat moorings. But for years controversy has been raging about whether Minas Basin in Nova Scotia or Leaf Basin in Quebec has boasting rights to this record. Finally, in 2005, three experts from the Canadian Hydrographic Service determined to resolve the issue once and for all. Their study showed that, while the highest tide measured in the Minas Basin was 4in (0.1m) higher than the highest tide in the Leaf Basin, neither set of measurements was completely reliable. As the margin of error was ±15in (0.4m), they concluded the results were the same and declared a draw. The battle isn't over yet, however. The next set of extreme high tides are expected in 2014, for which the predicted results are: Minas Basin 56ft (17m), Leaf Basin 55ft (16.8m) – still within the ±15in (0.4m) margin of error. Tidal gauges at the ready.

MOSKSTRAUMEN

It's been immortalised in stories by the likes of Edgar Allan Poe, Jules Verne and Herman Melville, as well as in Old Norse poetry and paintings. The Moskstraumen maelstrom in northern Norway is certainly an impressive beast, running at speeds of up to 17.27mph (27.79km/h). Unlike most other maelstroms, which are giant whirlpools that are usually found in narrow straits or passages, the Moskstraumen is formed by a convergence of currents that meet in the open sea between Lofoten Point and the island of Mosken. Poe's depiction of the phenomenon in his short story 'A Descent into the Maelstrom' introduced the word maelstrom into the English language and cemented the legacy of 'the most terrible hurricane that ever came out of the heavens'. Surprisingly, however, Moskstraumen isn't the strongest current in the world. That honour goes to the Saltstraumen Maelstrom which is just a few miles further south. This has been known to clock up current speeds of a rip-roaring 25mph (40km/h).

The worst maelstroms in the world (current speed)

Saltstraumen Maelstrom, Bodø, Norway 25mph (40km/h)

Moskstraumen Maelstrom, Lofoten Islands, Norway 17.27mph (27.79km/h)

Old Sow Whirlpool, Deer Island, New Brunswick, Canada 17.15mph (27.60km/h)

Skookumchuck Narrows, British Columbia, Canada 16mph (26km/h)

Naruto Whirlpool, Naruto Strait, Japan .... 12mph (20 km/h)

POE'S MAELSTROM

'When it is flood, the stream runs up the country between Lofoden and Moskoe with a boisterous rapidity; but the roar of its impetuous ebb to the sea is scarce equalled by the loudest and most dreadful cataracts; the noise being heard several leagues off, and the vortices or pits are of such an extent and depth, that if a ship comes within its attraction, it is inevitably absorbed and carried down to the bottom, and there beat to pieces against the rocks; and when the water relaxes, the fragments thereof are thrown up again.'

Source: *A Descent into the Maelstrom* by Edgar Allan Poe, 1841

VERNE'S MAELSTROM

'The maelstrom! The maelstrom! Could a more dreadful word in a more dreadful situation have sounded in our ears! We were then upon the dangerous coast of Norway. [...] We knew that at the tide the pent-up waters between the islands of Ferroe and Loffoden rush with irresistible violence, forming a whirlpool from which no vessel ever escapes. From every point of the horizon enormous waves were meeting, forming a gulf justly called the "Navel of the Ocean", whose power of attraction extends to a distance of twelve miles. There, not only vessels, but whales are sacrificed, as well as white bears from the northern regions.'

Source: *Twenty Thousand Leagues Under the Sea* by Jules Verne, 1869

The worst tsunamis in the world (deaths)

Indian Ocean, 2004 350,000	Tokaido-Nankaido, Japan, 1707 30,000
Messina, Italy, 1908 123,000	Arica, Chile, 1868 25,674
Lisbon, Portugal, 1755 100,000	Sanriku, Japan, 1896 22,000
South China Sea, 1782 40,000	Tohoku, Japan, 2011 16,000
Krakatoa, Indonesia, 1883 36,500	Kyushu Island, Japan, 1792 15,030

THE BIRTH OF METEOROLOGY

ADMIRAL ROBERT FITZROY is best known as the captain of HMS *Beagle* during Charles Darwin's voyage to Patagonia in 1831–36. After returning to England, he wrote and edited the first two volumes of the three-part account of the voyage, with Darwin authoring the third. But Fitzroy was also a keen meteorologist and, after setting up what would eventually become the Meteorological Office, he invented a variety of affordable barometers that were installed in harbours around the country to help fishermen predict the weather. He then established a network of data-collecting stations that enabled him to issue the first weather forecasts in the land. In recognition of the many lives he saved with his work, the sea area of Finisterre in the British shipping forecast was renamed Fitzroy.

THE WINDY ZONE

'Below the Roaring Forties there is no law;
Below the Furious Fifties there is no God.'

It's the warm winds flowing down from the Equator meeting the cold air from Antarctica that, combined with the rotation of the Earth, create the unique weather conditions of the Southern Ocean. Undeflected by any land mass, the winds blow unabated (averaging 40–50mph/65–80km/h), and the seas build and build (40ft/12m waves are not uncommon). Not for nothing were these regions known as the Roaring Forties (40–49 degrees south), Furious Fifties (50–59 degrees south) and Screaming Sixties (60–69 degrees south), giving rise to the above adage. Sailors who knew how to make the most of these conditions sailed to Sydney via the Cape of Good Hope in as little as 72 days (*Cutty Sark*'s record) and home via Cape Horn in as little as 77 days (*Thermopylae*'s record). Modern racing yachts use essentially the same route to make their record-breaking journeys – the current non-stop round-the-world record being 45 days (crewed) and 57 days (single-handed).

Weather lore 2

'Mare's tails and mackerel scales
Make tall ships take in their sails.'

Too true! The mare's tails are high cirrus clouds, while the mackerel scales
are cirrocumulus – both suggesting the approach of a front.
Tall ships and small ships alike take heed.

BLOW WIND BLOW

One man's gale is another's man's breeze. This was the dilemma that Sir Francis Beaufort, a British admiral and hydrographer, set out to resolve when he created his wind scale in 1805. Because there was no way of measuring wind speed, he used visual observation to create 13 categories, ranging from 0 to 12. And, because it was devised for the Royal Navy, the observations were based on the amount of sail a man-of-war could carry. These ranged from 'just sufficient to give steerage' to 'that which no canvas sails could withstand'. By 1906, the descriptions were replaced by how the sea looked. Later, with the advent of anemometers, a formula was invented to create 'miles per hour' readings.

The Beaufort Scale

Force	Wind speed: Knots (m/s)	Max wave height (m)	Wind description	Sea description
0	>1 (> 1)	0	Calm	Sea is like a mirror
1	1–3 (1–2)	0.1	Light air	Ripples with appearance of scales; no foam crests
2	4–6 (2–3)	0.3	Light breeze	Small wavelets; crests of glassy appearance, not breaking
3	7–10 (4–5)	1	Gentle breeze	Large wavelets; crests begin to break; scattered whitecaps
4	11–16 (6–8)	1.5	Moderate breeze	Small waves, becoming longer; numerous whitecaps
5	17–21 (9–11)	2.5	Fresh breeze	Moderate waves, taking longer form; many whitecaps; some spray
6	22–27 (11–14)	4	Strong breeze	Larger waves forming; whitecaps everywhere; more spray
7	28–33 (14–17)	5.5	Near gale	Sea heaps up; white foam from breaking waves begins to be blown in streaks
8	34–40 (17–21)	7.5	Gale	Moderately high waves of greater length; edges of crests begin to break into spindrift; foam is blown in well–marked streaks
9	41–47 (21–24)	10	Severe gale	High waves; sea begins to roll; dense streaks of foam; spray may begin to reduce visibility
10	48–55 (25–28)	12.5	Storm	Very high waves with overhanging crests; sea takes white appearance as foam is blown in very dense streaks; rolling is heavy and visibility is reduced
11	56–63 (29–32)	16	Violent storm	Exceptionally high waves; sea covered with white foam patches; visibility further reduced
12	64+ (33+)	16+	Hurricane	Air filled with foam; sea completely white with driving spray; visibility greatly reduced

FIZZING IN THE RIGGING

It can be tempting to dismiss the sailors of yesteryear as superstitious folk who believed in all sorts of silly omens and were ignorant of science. But it would take a very rational person indeed not to believe in magic when, in the midst of an ocean thunderstorm, the tips of your ship's masts start fizzing and glowing with an unearthly blue light. This is the phenomenon known as St Elmo's fire, which has been reported by figures as varied as Julius Caesar, Pliny the Elder, Magellan, Columbus, Richard Henry Dana and many lesser-known sailors. The scientific explanation is an imbalance in electrical charge. During a thunderstorm, both clouds and ship become electrically charged. This wouldn't normally be visible, but because the current is concentrated in the extremities of objects such as masts and booms (or lamp-posts and antennae on shore) and because the atmosphere is more conducive to carrying an electrical current, the air around them becomes ionised. The object then glows slightly to produce St Elmo's fire. It's essentially the same as what happens in a fluorescent light tube – except it's happening up in your rigging in the middle of an ocean. No wonder sailors thought it was magic.

Shakespeare's Fire

'I boarded the Kings' ship; now in the beak,
Now in the waist, the deck, in every cabin,
I flamed amazement; sometime I'd divide
And burn in many places; on the topmast
The yards and bowsprit, would I flame distinctly
Then meet and join.'

Source: Words of Ariel in *The Tempest*, Act I, Scene 2, by William Shakespeare

WEATHER LORE 3

'Wind before rain, let your topsail fill again.
Rain before wind, sheets and topsails mind.'

Wind before rain may be caused by localised showers, suggesting it will blow over soon. If the rain comes before the wind, however, it's probably from an approaching front and signals there will be unsettled weather for a day or two.

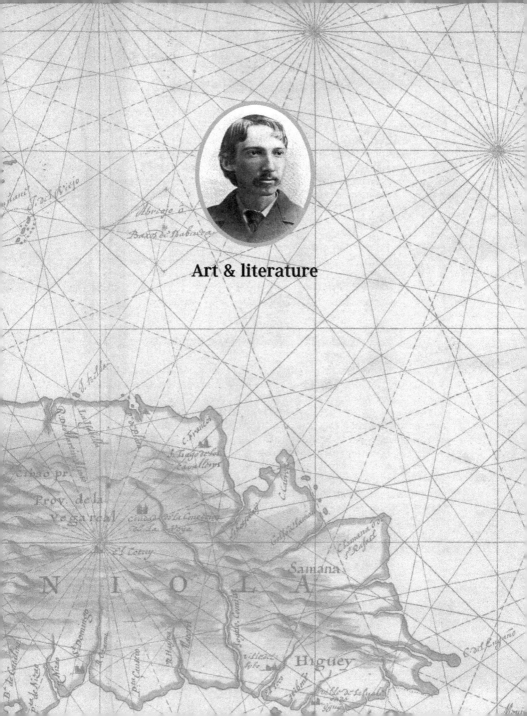

Art & literature

THE SAILOR WHO COULDN'T READ

Pierre Loti (real name, Julien Viaud) was a serving officer in the French Navy when he wrote his first, semi-autobiographical novel *Aziyadé* in 1879. Based on his love affair with a harem girl from Constantinople, it introduced readers to many of the themes that would characterise his later work: exotic locations, indigenous people and risqué sexual situations. His next book, *Le Marriage de Loti*, was set in Tahiti and also concerned his affair with a local girl. But it was his description of the atrocities meted out by the French forces to the Vietnamese during the Battle of Thuan, published in *Le Figaro* in 1883, that gave him national notoriety and almost got him dismissed from the navy. In fact, he went on to have a long career at sea, and was eventually promoted to captain. His 1886 novel *An Iceland Fisherman*, describing the lives of Breton fishermen, became a classic of French literature, and Loti was elected to the Académie Française in 1891. Always one to fan the flames of controversy, he told the Académie, 'Loti ne sait pas lire' ('Loti can't read'), although his prodigious literary output and personal library told otherwise.

AN ARTIST AND HIS OCEAN GARRET

Winslow Homer is now recognised as one of the giants of American art, and is arguably the most famous American marine artist ever. But 'twas not ever thus. When his iconic painting *Breezing Up* was first exhibited in 1876, the author Henry James gave it and other paintings by Homer a very mixed review, saying: 'We frankly confess that we detest his subjects... he has chosen the least pictorial range of scenery and civilization; he has resolutely treated them as if they were pictorial... and, to reward his audacity, he has incontestably succeeded.' Homer's subject matter would become more gritty and his palette more sober as he recorded the lives of working people both in the USA and the UK. Even when he received critical acclaim, sales of his paintings remained sluggish, with some of his major works fetching as little as $400. In his mid-50s, Homer still looked to his brother Charles for support, and it wasn't until his 60s that he finally achieved some degree of financial stability. Nowadays, Homer's oils sell for up to £50m ($30m), and his watercolour *The Red Canoe* sold for £8m ($4.8m), a record for an American watercolour.

> ❝ The sea, the snotgreen sea, the scrotumtightening sea. ❞
>
> *Ulysses* by James Joyce, 1922

ROBINSON CRUSOE WAS A CAPITALIST

You might think *Robinson Crusoe* was a tale about a shipwrecked sailor who fetches up on an island off South America and has to live by his wits until rescue arrives. Well, think again. Daniel Defoe's 1719 story has been seized upon by economists as varied as David Ricardo and Karl Marx to illustrate certain types of economic systems. According to the classical school of economics, the book highlights a primitive form of capitalism, whereby Crusoe must make choices between production and leisure. When Friday appears on the scene, the benefits of trade are revealed. To Marx, the story demonstrates the superiority of labour over capital. There are many other interpretations, including colonial and religious ones. And don't even get me started on the feminist analysis...

Bestselling fictional sea adventure stories

The Old Man and the Sea by Ernest Hemingway

The Mauritius Command by Patrick O'Brian

Treasure Island by Robert Louis Stevenson (right)

Post Captain by Patrick O'Brian

Mr Midshipman Hornblower by CS Forester

Admiral Hornblower in the West Indies by CS Forester

Lieutenant Hornblower by CS Forester

The Truelove by Patrick O'Brian

Hornblower and the Atropos by CS Forester

Hornblower and the Hotspur (Vol. 3) by CS Forester

Source: Amazon.com bestseller list, 11 October 2012

THE BEST (SEA) PAINTING

ACCORDING TO A POLL conducted by the BBC, JMW Turner's 1839 painting *The Fighting Temeraire* is 'the greatest painting in Britain'. The picture depicts the HMS *Temeraire*, which played a critical role in the Battle of Trafalgar, being towed up the River Thames by a steam tug to be broken up at the end of her career. At the time, it was interpreted as a nostalgic commentary on the end of the age of sail and the triumph of steam power. The painting received 27% of the total votes cast in the poll. Runners-up were: *The Hay Wain* by Constable (18 per cent), *A Bar at the Folies-Bergère* by Manet (11 per cent), *The Arnolfini* by Jan van Eyck (9 per cent), *Mr and Mrs Clark and Percy* by Hockney (7 per cent) and *Sunflowers* by Van Gogh (7 per cent).

HORROR BECOMES ART

A CAPTAIN PAST HIS PRIME, too few lifeboats and preference given to the privileged – sound familiar? No, it's not the *Titanic*, but the *Médusa*, a French naval frigate that ran aground off what is now Mauritania in 1816. The ship was on its way to Senegal with the new French governor Colonel Schmaltz and his wife, under terms agreed by the newly restored French king, Louis XVIII. The ship's captain was one Vicomte de Chaumareys, who hadn't sailed a ship in 20 years but was given the command through political nepotism. The *Médusa* was carrying 400 people on board when it went aground, but only had lifeboats for 250. The rest had to content themselves with a raft built from scraps of timber dismantled from the ship. During the 13 days that followed, most died of starvation, were killed and eaten by their comrades, or threw themselves into the sea to drown. Only 15 of the original 150 survived. The incident was a massive embarrassment to the French government but made a certain young painter's reputation when he turned it into a dramatic painting. *The Raft of the Médusa* (below) by Théodore Géricault is widely regarded as one of France's finest paintings and is exhibited at the Louvre Gallery in Paris. His fellow painter Eugène Delacroix is said to have modelled for one of the figures (the man in the foreground with arms stretched down). As for Captain de Chaumareys and Mr and Mrs Schmaltz, they all made it ashore on the lifeboats – although de Chaumareys was sentenced to three years in prison for incompetence and cowardice.

'BARNACLE BILL THE SAILOR'

'Who's that knocking at my door?' (repeated three times)
Cried the fair young maiden.
'It's only me from over the sea,' says Barnacle Bill the sailor.
'I'm all lit up like a Christmas tree,' says Barnacle Bill the sailor.
'I'll sail the sea until I croak,
I fight and swear and drink and smoke,
But I can't swim a bloomin' stroke,
I'm Barnacle Bill the Sailor.'

'Are you young and handsome, sir?'(x3)
Cried the fair young maiden.
'I'm old and rough and dirty and tough,' says Barnacle Bill the sailor.
'I never can get drunk enough,' says Barnacle Bill the sailor.
'I drink my whisky when I can, whisky from an old tin can,
For whisky is the life of man,
I'm Barnacle Bill the Sailor.'

'I'll come down and let you in,' (x3)
Cried the fair young maiden.
'Well, hurry before I bust in the door,' says Barnacle Bill the sailor.
'I'll rare and tear and rant and roar,' says Barnacle Bill the sailor.
'I'll spin you yarns and tell you lies, I'll drink your wine and eat your pies,
I'll pinch your cheeks and black your eyes,
I'm Barnacle Bill the Sailor.'

'Sing me a love song low and sweet,' (x3)
Said the fair young maiden.
'Sixteen men on a dead man's chest,' says Barnacle Bill the sailor.
'Yo, ho, ho, and a bottle of rum,' says Barnacle Bill the sailor.
'Oh, high jig-a-jig on the rolling sea, and a hi and a ho, you're the gal for me,
Hoorah, me boys, for the Nancy Lee,
I'm Barnacle Bill the Sailor.'

'Tell me that we soon shall wed,' (x3)
Cried the fair young maiden.
'I've got me a wife in every port,' says Barnacle Bill the sailor.
'The handsome gals is what I court,' says Barnacle Bill the sailor.
'With my false heart and flattering tongue,
I courts 'em all both old and young,
I courts 'em all, but marries none,
I'm Barnacle Bill the Sailor.'

Source: From the cartoon *Barnacle Bill*, directed by Dave Fleischer, 1930

ODYSSEUS'S ROUTE(S)

There's little agreement on the route taken by Odysseus in Homer's *Odyssey*, or even if any of the locations correspond to real places. One of the most convincing interpretations was offered by the French diplomat Victor Bérard. It goes like this:

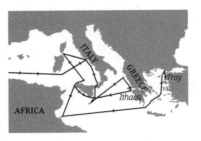

TROY: Most scholars agree the starting point of the Odyssey was a real place located on the Aegean coast of Turkey. It's now a UNESCO World Heritage site.

LAND OF THE LOTUS EATERS: According to Bérard, Odysseus's men go in search of food on the island of Djerba off Tunisia. Others place this incident in Libya.

LAND OF THE CYCLOPES: The one-eyed monster lives in Posillo, Italy, now Naples. Others say Sicily or the Balearics.

AEOLIA: Odysseus is given the bag of winds on the island of Stromboli, north of Sicily. Others claim Aeolia was Lipari, in the same group of islands.

LAND OF THE LAESTRYGONIANS: The cannibals inhabit northern Sardinia. Others say south-east Sicily.

AEAEA: Circe cast her magic spells at Monte Circeo, between Naples and Rome. Others claim it was Ischia or Madeira.

ENTRANCE TO THE UNDERWORLD: Odysseus finds the prophet Tiresias at Cumae, near Naples. Others suggest the River Rhine, or even South America.

THE SIRENS: Odysseus hears the Sirens' bewitching song off the coast of Lucania, southern Italy. Author Tim Severin places the incident in Levkas, Greece.

SCYLLA AND CHARYBDIS: The six-headed monster and the whirlpool are on either side of the Strait of Messina in Italy. Or perhaps the Bay of Fundy in Canada?

THRINACIA/HELIOS: Odysseus's surviving crew are all killed at what Bérard identifies as Sicily. Others say it's Malta.

OGYGIA: Odysseus's seven-year affair with Calypso takes place in the Straits of Gibraltar. Other contenders are: Malta, the Ionian Sea, Egypt or the Atlantic.

SCHERIA/PHAEACIA: The home of the friendly Phaeacians is said by Bérard and others to be Corfu (or Corcyra).

ITHACA: Odysseus returns home after his ten-year odyssey to what Bérard says is the real Ithaca. Others contend it's the islands of Levkas or Cephalonia.

❛ I must be a mermaid, Rango.
I have no fear of depths and a great fear of shallow living. ❜

Anaïs Nin, French-Cuban author (1903–1977)

Sir Robin Knox-Johnston's Desert Island Discs

'Swinging Safari' by Bert Kaempfert

'As Some Day It May Happen' from *The Mikado* by Gilbert and Sullivan

Symphony No. 5 in C minor by Ludwig van Beethoven

'Stranger on the Shore' by Acker Bilk

'Loudly Let the Trumpets Bray' from *Iolanthe* by Gilbert and Sullivan

'All You Need Is Love' by the Beatles

'Jesu, Joy of Man's Desiring' from Cantata No. 147 by JS Bach

Pomp and Circumstance March No. 1 in D major, 'Land of Hope and Glory', by Edward Elgar

Sir Robin Knox-Johnston was the first man to sail around the world singlehanded non-stop in 1968. Desert Island Discs, 4 July 1970

THE REAL 'MARK TWAIN'

The American author Samuel L. Clemens was a printer, a ship's pilot and a miner before he took up journalism in the mid-1860s. While working as a pilot on the River Mississippi, he heard the phrase 'mark twain' called out by the crew measuring the depth of the water with a lead line. The line was marked at every fathom (about 6ft/1.8m), so when the second (or 'twain') fathom was reached, the leadsman would call out 'mark twain' to the helmsman. Clemens used the pseudonym Mark Twain for the first time in 1863, and achieved national fame for 'The Celebrated Jumping Frog of Calaveras County', which he wrote in 1865. He achieved worldwide recognition with *The Adventures of Tom Sawyer* (1876), based on his childhood by the Mississippi, and its sequel *The Adventures of Huckleberry Finn* (1885), often described as 'the Great American Novel'.

KON-TIKI AT NO. 1

IT WAS AN AUDACIOUS PLAN: to build a replica of a 5th-century balsa raft and sail 5,000 miles (8,000km) across the Pacific with no instruments other than a VHF radio. Thor Heyerdahl's plan was to prove the Pacific islands could have been populated by people from South America, and not just from the Asian mainland as previously thought. After 101 days at sea, during which he and his four crew survived by catching sharks, the *Kon-Tiki* crashed on a reef at Raroia in the Tuamotu Islands on 7 August, 1947. Heyerdal had proven his point – although the scientific establishment remained unconvinced. He struggled to find a publisher for his book, but *The Kon-Tiki Expedition*, finally published in 1945, went on to become one of the bestselling maritime books ever.

[Cooper] loved the sea and looked at it with consummate understanding. [...] His descriptions have the magistral ampleness of a gesture indicating the sweep of a vast horizon. They embrace the colours of sunset, the peace of starlight, the aspects of calm and storm, the great loneliness of the waters, the stillness of watchful coasts, and the alert readiness which marks men who live face to face with the promise and the menace of the sea. He knows the men and he knows the sea. His method may be often faulty, but his art is genuine. The truth is within him.

Tales of the Sea by Joseph Conrad, 1898

CAPSIZING TO MUSIC

A SAILOR TRAPPED in his capsized yacht in the Southern Ocean might seem an unlikely story to set to music. But this is exactly what the modern composer Roxanna Panufnik has done in her piece *The Upside Down Sailor*, released in 2003. The 51-minute set describes the experience of British sailor Tony Bullimore when his boat capsized during the 1997 Vendée Globe race. The story of the 'upside-down sailor' made worldwide headlines and delighted viewers when he was found alive after five days in the slowly sinking vessel. Panufnik has created an evocative score in 14 parts, accompanied by a stirring narrative by Richard Stilgoe (better known for his lyrics in *Starlight Express* and *The Phantom of the Opera*). It's not exactly *The Marriage of Figaro*, but it's certainly different.

Clare Francis's Desert Island Discs

La Mer by Claude Debussy
'Dance of the Knights' from *Romeo and Juliet* by Sergey Prokofiev
'The Peanut Vendor' by the Original Trinidad Steel Band
'C'est à Hambourg' by Édith Piaf
'Vesti la Giubba' from *Pagliacci* by Ruggero Leoncavallo
Symphony No. 4 In E minor by Johannes Brahms
'Doina de Jale' by Gheorghe Zamfir
Organ Symphony No. 5 in F minor by Charles-Marie Widor

Clare Francis was the first woman skipper in several prominent ocean races in the 1970s. Desert Island Discs, 9 July 1977

Dame Ellen MacArthur's Desert Island Discs

'Hey Ya' by OutKast
'The Boys of Summer' by Don Henley
'I Wish It Would Rain Down' by Phil Collins
'Me Gustas Tu – I Like You' by Manu Chao
'Any Other Name' by Thomas Newman
'Here With Me' by Dido
'Through the Barricades' by Spandau Ballet
'Fix You' by Coldplay

Dame Ellen MacArthur broke the record for sailing around the world singlehanded in 2005. Desert Island Discs, 4 October 2009

THE FIRST SEA NOVEL?

The American writer James Fenimore Cooper may be best known for his novel *The Last of the Mohicans*, but it is two other lesser-known books that are most treasured by sailing folk. In *The Pilot* and *The Red Rover*, Cooper depicted life at sea in a way no other writer before him had done and created a new genre of literature: the sea novel. For, while Tobias Smollett and others included nautical scenes in their stories, Cooper's books put ships and the sea at the centre of the action and depicted sailors as three-dimensional human beings rather than mere stereotypes. In *The Pilot*, a character based on the American War of Independence hero John Paul Jones leads daring attacks on the English enemy, while *The Red Rover* introduces the reader to a world of pirates and slaves in pursuit of freedom from English oppressors. Both books are packed with old salts and authentic nautical scenes (Cooper served in the American Navy for several years) but these are used to talk about more general themes, such as race, liberty and the nature of warfare. Nine more sea novels would follow.

A mountain is composed of tiny grains of earth. The ocean is made up of tiny drops of water. Even so, life is but an endless series of little details, actions, speeches, and thoughts. And the consequences whether good or bad of even the least of them are far-reaching.

Swami Sivananda, Hindu spiritual teacher (1887–1963)

IN THE BEGINNING

A hundred years before James Fenimore Cooper and 200 years before CS Forester and Patrick O'Brian, there was Tobias Smollett.

A former surgeon's mate in the Royal Navy, Smollett was the first writer to feature ships and the sea extensively in his novels – although it would be an exaggeration to regard them as pure sea novels. He made his name with *The Adventures of Roderick Random* (1748), which tells the tale of a Scottish gent who is ostracised by his family and travels the world living by his wits. He serves first on a British privateer and is later press-ganged into service with the Royal Navy, and Smollett gives graphic descriptions of both. He also tackles such topical themes as slavery, homosexuality, prostitution, class, corruption and greed. The book is a classic picaresque novel, in the vein of Henry Fielding's *Tom Jones*, published a year later.

SOAPSUDS AND WHITEWASH

STORMS AT SEA ARE NOTORIOUSLY DIFFICULT to capture convincingly on canvas. One way to overcome this problem, JMW Turner decided, was to go out in a storm lashed to the mast of a ship. The result was *Snow Storm*, which depicts a steamship struggling in the vortex of a tremendous gale, possibly off the coast of Harwich, in Essex. According to the Victorian art critic John Ruskin, Turner said of the painting: 'I did not paint it to be understood, but I wished to show what such a scene was like; I got the sailors to lash me to the mast to observe it; I was lashed for four hours, and I did not expect to escape, but I felt bound to record it if I did.' The painting was too abstract for the audience of the time, who complained they couldn't see where the harbour wall began or where it ended and dismissed the dramatic swirls of sea and cloud as 'soapsuds and whitewash'.

> ❝ Before me something appeared, something sombre and noisy, which had loomed up from all sides at once, and which seemed to have no end, a moving expanse which struck me with mortal vertigo [...] Above was stretched out full a sky all of one piece, of a dark gray colour like a heavy mantle, very, very far away, in unmeasurable depths of horizon, could be seen a break, an opening between sea and sky, a long empty crack, of a light pale yellow. ❞
>
> Introduction to *An Iceland Fisherman* by Pierre Loti (English version, 1902)

A man that is born falls into a dream like a man who falls into the sea. If he tries to climb out into the air as inexperienced people endeavour to do, he drowns.

Lord Jim by Joseph Conrad, 1900

CONRAD AT SEA

JOSEPH CONRAD is rightly revered as one of the world's finest writers – but he was a sailor first. Aged 17, Józef Korzeniowski, as he was then called, left his native Cracow and boarded a ship in Marseille. He spent nearly four years working on French ships, including a possible gun-running trip to the West Indies that provided the material for his novel *Nostromo*. He joined a British ship in 1878, to avoid conscription in France, and sailed on British ships for the next 16 years. A disastrous journey to the Far East in 1881 became the short story 'Youth', while a commission on the *Narcissus* in Bombay provided the basis of the novel *Nigger of the Narcissus*. More adventures at sea followed, including one in which Conrad assumed command after the captain died at sea and almost lost his whole crew to fever after it emerged the captain had sold the medicine he needed to cure them. Conrad turned these experiences into classic stories of the sea such as *Lord Jim* and *Typhoon*. Perhaps the most affecting of all, however, was his 1889 trip to the Congo that resulted in *Heart of Darkness* – and almost destroyed Conrad emotionally and physically.

Sir Francis Chichester's Desert Island Discs

'The Blue Danube Waltz' by Johann Strauss II
'Blue Room' by Bruce Trent
'Singin' in the Rain' by Ukelele Ike and Cliff Edwards
'Dojoji' by the Azuma Kabuki Musicians
Orpheus in the Underworld by Jacques Offenbach
Swan Lake, Act 2 by Pyotr Ilych Tchaikovsky
'Some Enchanted Evening' by Ezio Pinza
Piano Concerto No. 5 in E flat major, 'Emperor'
by Ludwig van Beethoven

Sir Francis Chichester was the first man to sail around the world singlehanded with one stop in 1967. Desert Island Discs, 23 October 1961

INDEX

INDEX & ACKNOWLEDGEMENTS

Acknowledgements

The publisher would like to thank the following for their kind permission to reproduce photographs in this book. (Abbreviations key: t = top, b = bottom, c = centre, r = right, l = left, bg = background)

Fotolia/AlienCat 2tl, 49tr; Fotolia/fireflamenco 3cl, 3bl, 60cl, 60br; Fotolia/Nautilus Krokodilius 5bl, 45, 53br; Fotolia/vector_master 22tl; Fotolia/Santi 28cr; Fotolia/laralova 28cl; Fotolia/ Erica Guilane-Nachez 86b; Fotolia/Carsten Reisinger 50cr; Fotolia/ msdesign 52tr; Fotolia/Kirill Semenov 56bl; Fotolia/cocoapapa 66b; Fotolia/makar 70cl istockphoto 6b, 55b

Library of Congress, Washington DC 4–5bg, 7bg, 19bg, 33bg, 45bg, 47br, 57bg, 65bg, 75bg, 83bg

Mary Evans/Interfoto/Sammlung Rauch 80tl

Wiki 14br, 18br, 30, 46tr, 75, 82tl

Artwork by John Woodcock and Ivan Hissey